THE FORGOTTEN JESUS

ROBBY GALLATY

LifeWay Press®
Nashville, Tennessee

Published by LifeWay Press® · © 2017 Robby Gallaty · Reprinted 2018

Material in this resource is adapted from *The Forgotten Jesus: How Western Christians Should Follow an Eastern Rabbi;* © 2017 Robby Gallaty; published by Zondervan, a division of HarperCollins Christian Publishing; Nashville, TN 37214. Used by permission.

ISBN 978-1-4627-4292-9 · Item 005793415

Dewey decimal classification: 232.95
Subject headings: JESUS CHRIST \ RABBIS \ JUDAISM—CUSTOMS AND PRACTICES

To order additional copies of this resource, write to LifeWay Resources Customer Service; One LifeWay Plaza; Nashville, TN 37234; fax 615-251-5933; phone toll free 800-458-2772; order online at LifeWay.com; email orderentry@lifeway.com; or visit the LifeWay Christian Store serving you.

Printed in the United States of America

Groups Ministry Publishing · LifeWay Resources · One LifeWay Plaza · Nashville, TN 37234

CONTENTS

ABOUT THE AUTHOR
ROBBY GALLATY

Robby Gallaty has served as the senior pastor of Long Hollow Baptist Church in Hendersonville, Tennessee, since 2015. He wasn't always a pastor, though.

For three years Robby battled a drug addiction that ravaged his life. A $180-a-day heroin and cocaine addiction drove him to steal $15,000 from his parents. After living without gas, electricity, and water for months; losing eight of his friends to drug-related deaths; watching six friends get arrested; and completing two rehabilitation treatments, Robby remembered the gospel that a friend shared with him in college and was radically saved on November 12, 2002.

Eight months later David Platt, a seminary student and church member at the time, asked Robby to meet weekly for accountability, prayer, and Bible study. For the next two years David instilled a passion for missions, expository preaching, and disciple making in Robby's life. He also encouraged Robby to go back to school to pursue theological education.

Robby earned his master of divinity in expository preaching in 2007 and his PhD in preaching in 2011 from New Orleans Baptist Theological Seminary. Today Robby's gospel conviction and evangelistic zeal compel him to passionately make disciples who make disciples.

Robby is also the founder of Replicate Ministries and the author of several books, including *Growing Up, Here and Now, Rediscovering Discipleship,* the LifeWay Bible study *Knowing Jesus,* and the chronological Bible-reading resources *Foundations* and *Foundations: New Testament.*

Robby and his wife, Kandi, have two sons: Rig and Ryder.

HAMILTON BARBER helped develop and write the content for this Bible study. Hamilton works as a content writer and an editor at Long Hollow Baptist Church. He holds a BA in English from the University of Tennessee in Chattanooga. Hamilton has edited books and Bible studies for Replicate Ministries and self-published a volume of poetry in 2017. He and his wife, Morgan, live in Hendersonville, Tennessee.

HOW TO USE THIS STUDY

This Bible study provides a guided process for individuals and small groups to examine Jesus' historical, cultural, and religious context as an Eastern rabbi. This study follows a six-week format that examines these topics:

Week 1: Considering Jesus' Jewishness

Week 2: Jesus' Childhood

Week 3: Jesus' Teaching Ministry

Week 4: Messianic Miracles

Week 5: The Last Week

Week 6: Words from the Cross

Each week is divided into two days of personal study. In these studies you'll find biblical teaching and interactive questions that will help you understand and apply Jesus' words and teachings from a Hebrew mindset.

In addition to the personal study, six group sessions are provided that are designed to spark conversations based on brief video teachings. Each group session is divided into three sections:

1. "Start" focuses participants on the topic of the session's video teaching.
2. "Watch" provides key ideas presented in the video and space to take notes.
3. "Discuss" guides the group to respond to and apply the video teaching.

Consider going deeper in your study by reading the book on which this Bible study is based. *The Forgotten Jesus: How Western Christians Should Follow an Eastern Rabbi* (Zondervan) is ISBN 978-0-3105-2923-1.

DO YOU KNOW THE

JESUS

OF THE BIBLE?

INTRODUCTION

Jesus was a Jewish man who was raised in a Jewish culture, was reared by exceptionally devout Jewish parents, and lived according to Jewish laws. He was circumcised on the eighth day of His earthly life and was dedicated to the Lord. As Jesus grew up, He regularly attended the synagogue on the Sabbath, participated in every biblical feast, studied and memorized the Scriptures, learned a trade from His father, and started His rabbinic ministry at age thirty—all according to Jewish customs of the time.

At the age of thirty, Jesus selected and called twelve Jewish men to forsake everything, learn His teachings, and carry on His mission. Consequently, prior to His death, most of Jesus' followers were Jews who professed faith in Him as the Messiah but still celebrated the Jewish festivals, worshiped in the temple, and observed the Sabbath.

If we look at Christianity today and compare it to the way it began, we might notice that the Jewishness of both its founder and its original followers has been lost. In this study we'll put ourselves in the shoes of the people who physically walked with Jesus. They observed His actions, heard His voice, lived in the same culture, and knew the same stories. Once we've put ourselves into the mindset of a Hebrew, we'll take a look at some of Jesus' teachings, which will come alive to us as never before.

I pray that through this Bible study you'll get to know Jesus—the historical, physical Jesus who walked and lived and breathed—and that you'll be changed by your encounter with Him.

WEEK 1

CONSIDERING JESUS' JEWISHNESS

START

Welcome to group session 1.
Use the following content to start the session.

Have you ever taken a painting class? One of the first things you're taught is to sketch your painting in pencil before breaking out the colors. This way you can make sure all the lines are in place, the shapes are where they need to be, and the outlines fit the picture you'll eventually create. This penciled outline is important because it lets you know where all of the colors need to go.

Do you prefer to outline, sketch, or plan something you write, draw, or say, or do you prefer to be more spontaneous?

In His most famous sermon Jesus said something we sometimes have difficulty understanding:

> *Don't think that I came to abolish the Law or the Prophets. I did not come to abolish but to fulfill.*
> **MATTHEW 5:17**

In the New Testament the Law and the Prophets refer to what we call the Old Testament. Jesus was saying that instead of abolishing or destroying the Old Testament Scriptures or setting them aside, He came to fulfill them—literally, to fill them full.

In many ways the Old Testament commandments can be understood as the pencil sketch of God's purposes, and Jesus is the proverbial paint. The full picture of who God was and what He was doing wasn't complete when God gave the Jewish people the law and established a relationship with them. He brought it to completion in the person of Jesus.

As we study Jesus in His historical, cultural, and religious context, we'll begin to see Him in a different light. In the process we'll learn how twenty-first-century Westerners can follow a first-century Eastern rabbi.

Watch and discuss video session 1.

WATCH

Jesus is saying, "I've come to fill it full. I've come to interpret it correctly."

Jesus isn't saying the order has been fulfilled. He's saying it's been interpreted correctly, in a way for you to understand it.

Westerners think on one hand. It has to be one or the other.

Easterners think on two hands.

You don't appreciate the New Testament because you don't understand the Old.

VIDEO SESSIONS AVAILABLE AT LIFEWAY.COM/FORGOTTENJESUS

DISCUSS

It's easy to operate from a mindset that reflects the culture we live in, especially when we talk about God. Jesus' culture often thought about God quite differently than we do.

What are some words you would use to describe God?

Do those words bring to mind any specific images for you? How do they help you see God more clearly?

Hebrew culture thought less in terms of dictionary words and more in terms of images or feelings.

Think of a picture that describes God. What do the characteristics of that image—such as smell, feel, and sound—say about God?

As we embark on a journey to rediscover an ancient Eastern rabbi as twenty-first-century Westerners, a useful starting point is to place ourselves in His context.

Why is it important to see Jesus through a Hebrew lens?

What are some examples of Greek thinking (A or B) and Hebrew thinking (A and B) in Scripture?

Developing a common understanding is often the first step in bringing two different cultures closer together. By learning how Jesus and the people around Him lived and thought, we'll be able to experience His teachings and understand His commands in a way that's both accurate and immediately applicable to our everyday lives.

How do you think studying Jesus' culture will help us better understand and obey His teachings?

READING PLAN

Read the following Scripture passages this week. Use the acronym HEAR and the space provided to record your thoughts or action steps.

DAY 1
Luke 2:1-24

DAY 2
Luke 2:25-52

DAY 3
Matthew 2

DAY 4
Mark 1:1-20

DAY 5
Mark 1:21-45

DAY 6
John 1:1-18

DAY 7
John 1:29-51

HIGHLIGHT · **E**XPLAIN · **A**PPLY · **R**ESPOND

REFLECT

During this study we'll walk together through Scripture to see Jesus' ministry in its proper context. When we discover the truth of God's Word for ourselves and let it take root in our hearts, it will change us.

For some people, the idea of studying Scripture by themselves is daunting. They feel they need special knowledge or a seminary degree to interpret and apply it. That couldn't be further from the truth. You can use a simple, four-step method called HEAR to clearly hear from God's Word.

THE HEAR METHOD

Explanation	*Example*
HIGHLIGHT	
As you're reading, select a passage from your reading to focus on.	"I am able to do all things through him who strengthens me" (Phil. 4:13).
EXPLAIN	
Examine the context of the verse. What do you think the purpose of this verse is in the context of the passage at large?	Paul told the church in Philippi that he had discovered the secret of contentment. No matter the situation, Paul realized that Christ was all he needed and that Christ would give him strength to persevere.
APPLY	
How does this passage speak to you personally? What action steps is it calling you to take? What condition of your heart is it correcting?	In life I'll experience many ups and downs. My contentment isn't found in circumstances. Rather, it's based on my relationship with Jesus. Only Jesus gives me the strength I need to be content in all of life.
RESPOND	
Record a prayer or commit to an action you can take in direct response to the passage.	Lord Jesus, please help me as I strive to be content in You. In Your strength I can endure any situation I must face.

As you work through this study over the coming week, use the HEAR journal to help you discover Scripture in a fresh way.

CUTTING A COVENANT

To Western, twenty-first-century ears, certain things in the Old Testament can seem foreign, bloody, and violent.

Read Genesis 15:9-11.

God came to Abram and initiated a covenant with him. God's instructions to Abram were specific. He was to bring five different animals that were to be killed in different ways. The beasts were to be killed and halved, and the birds were to be killed and left whole.

Think of what Abram was feeling as he brought these animals out to the site of the slaughter, as he was killing them, and as he was arranging them as God told Him to. It would have been a brutal scene, perhaps difficult to stomach. But God mandated this arrangement for a specific reason. Such an intentional act would have impressed Abram with the seriousness of the agreement to come.

Have you ever entered a serious agreement with someone?

**What did you do to let the person
know you were extremely serious?**

The preparation of the scene was also the preparation of Abram's heart. He knew by the end of it that God meant precisely what He was about to say: the covenant to come was sealed in blood, in sacrifice, and in gravity.

Interestingly, the preparation of this covenant was relatively standard in the ancient world. When two people wanted to seal a deal with each other, depending on the gravity of their agreement, the scene would be more or less bloody. Traditionally, after the preparation of this covenant ceremony was finished, both of the parties involved would step into the aisle of blood between the severed animals and say aloud to each other, "May what was done to these animals be done to me if I do not keep this covenant."[1]

At this point Abram was most likely feeling immense pressure. Not only had he prepared a ritual slaughter, but he was also about to enter a covenant with God—one that required both parties to be perfectly righteous. The only way Abram could uphold his end of this bargain was to be sinless—something he could never fulfill.[2]

When have you felt that you were in over your head?

How did you feel? In what way did your predicament appear impossible without God's intervention?

Read Genesis 15:12.

When the text tells us that Abram fell into a deep sleep that was accompanied with "great terror and darkness," it's using a Hebrew euphemism usually associated with death. Rather than signifying that Abram died, however, it signals to the reader that what came next was absolutely out of Abram's control. God, in His sovereignty, was making a deal he knew Abram stood no chance of fulfilling in his own power.

Verses 17-21 describe the rest of what happened. God, represented by a smoking pot and a flaming torch, moved between the elements of the covenant sacrifice. Because Hebrews think in pictures, we can rightly assume that both of these carried significant weight in a Hebrew's mind.

What's an item that carries special significance for you?

What does interacting with that item make you think of? Is it a memory, like a childhood heirloom? Is it an action, like a favorite baking dish?

M. G. Easton explains that this smoking pot "was a large pot, narrowing towards the top. When it was heated by a fire made within, the dough was spread over the heated surface, and thus was baked."[3]

Aided by the previous explanation, list images or feelings that come to mind when you think of a smoking, burning pot.

Where else do you see fire in Scripture? Why do you think God is associated with a consuming fire?

By bringing these three elements together—Abram's deep sleep, the burning pot, and the flaming torch—God was demonstrating that He would be the one responsible for keeping both sides of the agreement. Abram was a human like the rest of us. He sinned, struggled, and lived imperfectly, but those shortcomings didn't disqualify him from the promise God made to him in the covenant. He soon received his son Isaac and later became the father of many nations. All this happened because God took the responsibility for fulfilling His covenant promises.

Read Luke 22:20.

Under Abram humankind entered a covenant with God that was forged with the blood of sacrificed animals. Jesus ushered in a new covenant—this time forged with His own blood. God initiated this new covenant, provided the blood of His own Son, and upholds the terms of the covenant. All that's required of us to enter this covenant is faith in Christ. Through faith we accept that Christ fulfilled our portion of the covenant on the cross, and we allow ourselves to be covered by His sacrifice on our behalf.

What do you think is required for us to enter God's presence? How could we ever live up to that standard?

How did Jesus take up our end of the covenant the same way God took up Abram's? What ramifications does Jesus' fulfillment of the covenant have for your life today?

1. John Mark Hicks, *Come to the Table: Revisioning the Lord's Supper* (Orange, CA: New Leaf Books, 2002), 28.
2. Ray Vander Laan, *Prophets and Kings,* Faith Lessons, film (Israel: Ray Vander Laan, 1996).
3. M. G. Easton, *Illustrated Bible Dictionary* (New York: Cosimo, 2005), 269.

WHERE ARE YOU FROM?

This is one of those introductory questions we ask people we've just met because the answer tells us a lot about who the person is. If we meet someone from Zambia, for instance, we can assume they probably have an entirely different set of interests, tastes, and experiences from someone who was born in, say, Tennessee.

In the Hebrew tradition, though, where you're from refers to more than geographical location; it also refers to the people you're from. Who raised you says a lot about the way you were brought up and probably informs much of the way you think about and interact with the world.

Where are you from? What are your hometown and family like?

**What aspects of your personality do you think
are influenced by where and whom you're from?**

When Philip, one of the twelve disciples, first found Jesus, he found his friend Nathanael and said:

> *We have found the one Moses wrote about
> in the law (and so did the prophets):
> Jesus the son of Joseph, from Nazareth.*
> **JOHN 1:45**

There are two ways we can and should read Philip's introduction of Jesus as "the son of Joseph, from Nazareth." The first is fairly obvious: Jesus' father was Joseph, and they lived in Nazareth. But by being disconnected from the culture, we might miss the fact that "the son of Joseph" was a way rabbinic literature referred to the Messiah.[1]

Another Joseph is one of the most famous figures in the Old Testament. Try to list at least five key moments from Joseph's life.

Read about one key moment in Joseph's story:

Israel loved Joseph more than his other sons because Joseph was a son born to him in his old age, and he made a robe of many colors for him. When his brothers saw that their father loved him more than all his brothers, they hated him and could not bring themselves to speak peaceably to him. When Joseph came to his brothers, they stripped off Joseph's robe, the robe of many colors that he had on. Then they took him and threw him into the pit.
GENESIS 37:3-4,23-24

Joseph's rejection by his brothers is the first major turning point in his story. It sets the other parts in motion. Rejection is never easy to bear, but if we've been rejected, we're in good company. Many biblical heroes were rejected, among them Jesus Christ. Matthew 1:16 shows us something interesting about Jesus. His earthly father, Joseph, like the Old Testament Joseph, was the son of a man named Jacob. The Old Testament Jacob was renamed Israel by God. Just as his son Joseph was rejected by his brothers, Jesus was rejected by Israel's sons—the nation of Israel.

Describe a situation of rejection you've had to endure.

Explain how rejection could be used for God's glory or for your good.

After Joseph was sold into slavery in Egypt, he became a servant in the house of a man named Potiphar. Joseph eventually gained so much favor that he was put in charge of all of Potiphar's household. But all wasn't well yet.

Read Genesis 39:6-9,16-20.

Even in the face of great temptation, Joseph remained faithful to his master and to his morals. This fact is easy for us to see in hindsight, especially if we already know the end of this story. But we can't discount the pressure Joseph felt in that moment.

Take stock of your life. What's one sin that you would be most likely to give in to?

What are ways the enemy tempts you in this area?

What safeguards can you establish to keep from falling into that sin?

Joseph had a specific response to the temptation before him: he ran far away from it. In much the same way, Jesus experienced temptation from Satan himself. The enemy came to Him on three separate occasions in the desert, and each time Jesus had a specific response for him (see Matt. 4:1-11). Joseph avoided falling into temptation by fleeing; Jesus resisted temptation by quoting the Word of God.

When in prison for a crime he didn't commit, Joseph found himself in the company of a butler and a baker. The butler was eventually spared, while the baker was condemned (see Gen. 40). Similarly, when Jesus was sent to the cross, He was hung between two criminals—one of whom found salvation, the other of whom didn't.

One of the criminals hanging there began to yell insults at him: "Aren't you the Messiah? Save yourself and us!" But the other answered, rebuking him: "Don't you even fear God, since you are undergoing the same punishment? We are punished justly, because we're getting back what we deserve for the things we did, but this man has done nothing wrong." Then he said, "Jesus, remember me when you come into your kingdom." And he said to him, "Truly I tell you, today you will be with me in paradise."
LUKE 23:39-43

**Why do you think Jesus told only one of these
men that he would be with Him in paradise?**

What did the criminal do that made Jesus offer Him salvation?

The life of Joseph illustrates that he is a type of the Messiah, that is, a foreshadowing of the kind of person the Messiah would be. Though Joseph himself wasn't the savior of the world, he offered salvation to his family and other people during a famine (see Gen. 47). By this point Joseph had become second in command to Pharaoh. Because God told him a famine was coming, Joseph had prepared a massive amount of grain in storehouses, enough to sustain his entire kingdom and other people who came to him for help.

In an even more poignant way, Jesus provides nourishment that sustains for all eternity. Like Joseph's storehouses of grain, Jesus' provision can come through no other source.

What avenues to ultimate fulfillment does the world promise us?

In what ways does the world's fulfillment eventually run dry?

**How have you experienced dissatisfaction
with the world's promises?**

How has Jesus satisfied your soul's hunger?

Throughout the Old Testament and embedded in its culture lie shadows of the Messiah to come, all of which were realized in the person of Christ. As you come to know the real, historical Jesus, pray that He will reveal Himself to you more and more clearly so that you can follow Him passionately.

1. Roger Liebi, *The Messiah in the Temple* (Dusseldorf, Germany: Christlicher Medien-Vertrieb, 2003), 290.

WEEK 2

JESUS' CHILDHOOD

START

Welcome to group session 2.
Use the following content to start the session.

Last week we learned the difference between Western and Jewish ways of thinking.

**Can you summarize the difference
between the two perspectives?**

**What's an example of thinking like a Westerner
versus thinking like a Hebrew?**

When Kandi and I first started dating, one of the first things we talked about was our experiences growing up. When we hear about someone's upbringing, we're more likely to understand why they do certain things, why they find certain things important, and why they have a particular outlook on the world.

We can do the same thing with Jesus. Gospel writers, particularly Luke, preserved for us certain details of Jesus' upbringing. But remember that these writers were addressing people who were alive in the same time period as Jesus. Their readers knew the politics, the cultural conventions, and the events of an average lifetime in that day.

Through the years we've lost a sense of that time. We see a big gap in Jesus' earthly life—from age thirteen to about thirty—and it causes some people to speculate wildly about it. This speculation isn't necessary. From historical research we know what life was like for a Jewish boy growing up in first-century Israel. We can use that information to piece together what life may have looked like for young Jesus—what He did, how He was raised, and what schools of thought informed His teaching style. In doing so, we'll be able to understand His teachings with greater clarity and discern how they still relate deeply and personally to us today.

Watch and discuss video session 2.

WATCH

Mary knew the Word and loved the Word.

When a rabbi wanted to know if a student understood a doctrine
or theology, he would answer a question with a question.

Jesus is not asking questions because He needs insight. He is
answering with questions, and they are amazed at His understanding.

When we're trying to discern the truth of the Bible, we take into
consideration not only the language and the culture but also geography.

God today is still molding and shaping us
into the image of His Son, Jesus Christ.

Jesus Christ is not just a piece of our salvation. He's not just
a piece of our belief system. He is the centerpiece of everything.

VIDEO SESSIONS AVAILABLE AT LIFEWAY.COM/FORGOTTENJESUS

DISCUSS

**Take turns sharing something about your childhood
that influenced the way you live today.**

As we seek to know Jesus better, an important place to start is the context
in which He grew up. If we know the culture in which He was raised, it will help us
understand the images He chose, the examples He used when He was teaching,
and the way people would have understood what He was saying.

**What's something about Jesus' teachings or actions that
you could understand better by studying His upbringing?**

Why is it important to know the culture in which Jesus lived?

**Read aloud Matthew 16:18; 21:42; and 1 Peter 2:4-5.
If Jesus likely grew up working with stones as His father
did, how does that detail add clarity to these verses?
Why is it important to think of God as a rock?**

Even as a child, Jesus understood the importance of growing in love for the
Father by studying and obeying His Word.

What steps can you take to do the same thing today?

One of the most effective ways to grow in the Word is through discipleship—
an intentional time devoted to growing spiritually alongside other believers.

What does discipleship look like in your context?

**How can you help lead peers or coworkers in intentional times
of spiritual growth based on Jesus, the rock of our salvation?**

25

READING PLAN

Read the following Scripture passages this week. Use the acronym HEAR and the space provided to record your thoughts or action steps.

DAY 1
Psalm 1

DAY 2
Isaiah 28

DAY 3
Proverbs 4

DAY 4
Joshua 3

DAY 5
Joshua 4

DAY 6
Isaiah 40

DAY 7
Matthew 3

HIGHLIGHT · **E**XPLAIN · **A**PPLY · **R**ESPOND

REFLECT

Many of our thoughts and beliefs are rooted in the way we grew up. The values instilled in us as children provide a foundation on which the rest of our lives is built. We can pattern our lives after those formative influences or decide to live our lives differently. Christ gives us another option: He invites us to use Him as the foundation for our lives.

The Book of Proverbs has much to say about cultivating a home environment that's conducive to learning, wisdom, and discipline. Many of the proverbs were written by a father to sons, and most of them address relationships with God and others. One proverb begins like this: "Listen, sons, to a father's discipline, and pay attention so that you may gain understanding" (Prov. 4:1).

Home relations today are perhaps more tumultuous than ever. The American Psychological Association reports that between 40 and 50 percent of marriages end in divorce.[1] A Rutgers University study estimates that one in twenty-eight children has a parent in prison.[2] Twenty-one percent of children grow up in families whose incomes are below the poverty threshold.[3]

It's easy to look at statistics like these and worry about the kinds of homes in which the next generation is growing up. However, we're prepared for facing situations exactly like this. God laid out the plan to combat the world's efforts to destroy families. He instructed the fathers of Israel to repeat His commands to their children and thereby center their homes on His Word.

Scan Deuteronomy 6 and notice the steps God prescribed for establishing Israel's homes. Families were to center everything they did on His Word. Whether they were sitting or standing, coming or going, the Word of God was to be central.

**Evaluate your home when you were growing up.
What was the primary focus of your household?**

**What's the next step you can take
to devote your home to the Lord?**

1. American Psychological Association, "Marriage & Divorce," accessed June 26, 2017, www.apa.org/topics/divorce/.
2. Rutgers University, "Children and Families of the Incarcerated Fact Sheet," accessed June 26, 2017, https://nrccfi.camden.rutgers.edu/files/nrccfi-fact-sheet-2014.pdf.
3. National Center for Children in Poverty, "Child Poverty," accessed June 26, 2017, www.nccp.org/topics/childpoverty.html.

PERSONAL STUDY 1
SHEMA, ISRAEL

If you were like many people when you were growing up, you were flooded with advice from your parents. Someone who has lived through an experience naturally wants to offer advice to someone else who's about to start it—whether or not we like the advice.

In his book *Twelve Things I Want My Kids to Remember Forever*, Jerry B. Jenkins outlined some of the things he had learned the hard way with the hopes that his children wouldn't have to. Among them:

- Work before you play ... but make sure you play.
- Life isn't fair. So deal with it.
- Some people have the right to be wrong.
- Some things are black and white.[1]

What piece of advice made the greatest impact on you when you were growing up? Why?

Undoubtedly, Jenkins's kids didn't hear these pieces of advice for the first time when they read their father's book. He would have taught them these lessons one at a time as situations occurred in the life of the family.

God took the same approach with His children while they were in the wilderness of Israel. He wanted His people to base their lives on His Word, so He established a system to help them do just that. Soon after they departed Egypt, Moses ascended Mount Sinai, where God outlined the way His people were supposed to live according to His statutes. They would sojourn through areas controlled by people groups with drastically different ideas about creation, right and wrong, and how to treat one another. God intended for His people to be set apart, so He gave them the law to teach them how to live holy lives.

When you think of the law, what words come to mind?

What do you think the purposes of your country's laws are?

The Greek word *deuteronomion* is the root word that gave us the name of the fifth book of the Bible, Deuteronomy. It means "second law." But thinking about Deuteronomy as the second law doesn't necessarily summarize what the book says. Deuteronomy doesn't contain new information; rather, it contains God's words to His people that remind them, "As you move into a land of blessing, don't forget where you're from. Don't forget My instructions." For example, read this passage from Deuteronomy:

> *Listen, Israel: The L*ord *our God, the L*ord *is one. Love the L*ord *your God with all your heart, with all your soul, and with all your strength. These words that I am giving you today are to be in your heart. Repeat them to your children. Talk about them when you sit in your house and when you walk along the road, when you lie down and when you get up. Bind them as a sign on your hand and let them be a symbol on your forehead. Write them on the doorposts of your house and on your city gates.*
>
> **DEUTERONOMY 6:4-9**

For Jews, this is the most important passage in the Torah, the first five books of the Bible. It's so important, in fact, that it has a name—the *Shema*, which is the Hebrew word for "listen," the first word in the passage. The Shema does two things: it perfectly sums up the whole message of the law, and it provides a road map for how to live it.

Four essential ways to listen to the Word of God can be cited in this passage: remember, reflect, recite, repeat.

REMEMBER

"Listen, Israel: The LORD our God, the LORD is one. These words that I am giving you today are to be in your heart" (vv. 4,6). When Moses told the Israelites to listen, he was telling them to remember what God had taught them.

What's your earliest memory?

Record a time you remember God working in your life.

How did that experience help shape the way you think of God and the way He works?

Throughout their time in the desert, God instructed His children to remember what He was doing. One element in the tabernacle was the table that held the bread of the Presence. Twelve pieces of unleavened bread reminded the people of the nourishment God provided as they were wandering through the desert: God sent manna (like unleavened bread) and quail from heaven.

God also instructed the Israelites to build times of remembrance into their yearly calendars. Festivals held at regular intervals during the year served to remind the Israelites of certain major events in their lives. The Feast of Booths was established to remind the Israelites of the generation they spent living in tents (booths) in the desert. The Passover feast served to remind them of their successful evacuation from Egypt.

Many cultures have regular times of remembrance. Identify the event or people each of the following holidays commemorates.

Valentine's Day:

Easter:

Memorial Day:

Veteran's Day:

A memory can happen in a flash—a sudden recollection of something you had forgotten about—but that's not what God meant in Deuteronomy 6. Remembering is an intentional, specific action that can be carried out. We can see an example of the way God expected His children to remember in Joshua 3–4. When Moses died, Joshua took his place and prepared to take the Israelites into Canaan. But first they had to cross the Jordan River. Following God's instructions, priests carried the ark of the covenant into the Jordan. As soon as they did, the water stopped flowing, and the people crossed on dry land.

When they reached the other side, God instructed Joshua:

"Choose twelve men from the people, one man for each tribe, and command them: Take twelve stones from this place in the middle of the Jordan where the priests are standing, carry them with you, and set them down at the place where you spend the night." The Israelites did just as Joshua had commanded them. The twelve men took stones from the middle of the Jordan, one for each of the Israelite tribes, just as the LORD had told Joshua. They carried them to the camp and set them down there. Joshua also set up twelve stones in the middle of the Jordan where the priests who carried the ark of the covenant were standing. The stones are still there today.

JOSHUA 4:2-3,8-9

Because the Israelites had a famously short memory, God helped them out a little. Every time they saw those stones—which were still standing up to the time when the author wrote the Book of Joshua—they would remember the amazing things God had done to lead them into the promised land.

How can you set up "stone pillars" in your life that remind you to look back and remember what God has done for you?

How can looking back at your pillars encourage you to share the gospel with someone who needs to hear it?

Remembering something is simply bringing it to mind again. God wants us to recall frequently the things He has done for us. But remembering isn't only for our benefit.

REFLECT

People generally perform better if they follow a routine. Building time into our schedules for important things sets us on a path to get them done. God introduced the Sabbath to ensure that His people were basing their lives on His words and His works.

In Exodus 20:9-11 God set the Sabbath day apart from the rest of the days of the week and declared it holy. He built this weekly occurrence into the Israelite's schedules as an opportunity for them to reflect on ways He had sustained them through the previous week and to prepare spiritually for the week ahead. The Sabbath was designed to cultivate a state of mind that reflected on God's goodness:

> *You are to labor six days and do all your work, but the seventh*
> *day is a Sabbath to the LORD your God. You must not do any work—*
> *you, your son or daughter, your male or female servant, your*
> *livestock, or the resident alien who is within your city gates. For*
> *the LORD made the heavens and the earth, the sea, and everything*
> *in them in six days; then he rested on the seventh day. Therefore*
> *the LORD blessed the Sabbath day and declared it holy.*
> **EXODUS 20:9-11**

In your words, what was the purpose of the Sabbath?

Why do you think we often neglect this commandment today?

**What do you think we miss when we don't
observe a day of rest and reflection?**

When God created the universe, He didn't need to take a rest; He did so to model behavior for us because we need to rest. We're most at rest when we're quietly reflecting on what our God has done.

In Deuteronomy 6:4 God reminded the Israelites of an amazing truth: the Lord alone is God. God alone is God—not our deadlines, not our stresses, not our circumstances, not ourselves. Our reflections should point us to this truth.

With what objects and priorities do we replace God?

How can you put God back in His rightful place in your life?

When we make God the sole authority in our lives, we see and obey Him differently. As verse 5 says, we want to love Him with every fiber of our beings. Our love for God influences the way we interact with others, view situations around us, and regard ourselves. Right remembrance leads to worshipful reflection, which prepares you to share God's love and God's Word with the people in your life.

RECITE

Repeat them to your children. Talk about them when you sit in your house and when you walk along the road, when you lie down and when you get up. Bind them as a sign on your hand and let them be a symbol on your forehead. Write them on the doorposts of your house and on your city gates.
DEUTERONOMY 6:7-9

Our greatest opportunity to make disciples is with the people who live closest to us, and the only way we can make disciples who are passionately in love with the Lord is through His Word.

Describe your relationship with the person who's closest to you. What do you admire about this person? How do his or her strengths complement yours?

How has God worked in that relationship?

How can you use your "stone pillars" to talk with that person about ways God has worked in your life?

The people of Israel were not only to repeat God's Word to their children but also to proverbially bind His Word to their hands and foreheads and adorn their doorposts with it. As Judaism became a formal religion, devout Jews literally did this with phylacteries, leather boxes filled with Scriptures and bound to the arm and forehead. But you don't have to write Bible verses on your forehead or on your door; God was telling His people to keep His Word near them constantly in ways that would be instantly recognizable.

Have you ever met someone who exuded God's presence? What was it like to be around them?

Practically speaking, what do you think it looks like to wear God's Word on your sleeve or forehead?

Examine your life for a moment. What problem do you struggle with most?

How would keeping Scripture close to your heart throughout the day help you confront that issue?

REPEAT

God didn't intend for His instructions to be a one-time thing. They were to be the pattern of the Israelites' lives—to live a life soaked in God's Word, to let it flow from their mouths, and to allow it to increase their devotion to and love for the one true God.

Notice in Joshua 4 that the next generation would ask about the piles of rocks (see vv. 6-7). This would afford the people countless opportunities to repeat the story of God's action, cementing it in their minds and planting it in the minds of their children. Therefore, after reading the Word, we need to share it with our spouse, our friends, and our children.

God is the Father of truth, but repetition is the mother of all learning. God designed our brains to transfer information and solidify it in our minds at the same time.

What can you do to bathe yourself and your home with God's Word?

What's the next step you need to take in order to love God with everything you are?

1. Jerry B. Jenkins, *Twelve Things I Want My Kids to Remember Forever* (Chicago: Moody, 1991).

PERSONAL STUDY 2
A WALK TO REMEMBER

The Christian life is often called a walk, which is actually a good metaphor for the way the Christian life works. Walking is a methodical process; the same action is repeated over and over to propel us forward. If we start taking steps in the wrong direction, we have to take more steps in the right direction to get back on track to our destination. We can lay a solid foundation for our lives, but if we build on it unwisely, the building can still develop cracks.

Psalm 1 expresses the importance of walking correctly by using concrete images we can connect with. Let's look at the first two verses:

> *Blessed is the man*
> *who walks not in the counsel of the wicked.*
> **PSALM 1:1, ESV**

Have you ever walked on a treadmill? As the floor underneath your feet moves, you have to keep going forward in order to stay upright and not fall off the back. Even if you stop moving, the treadmill is going to keep going—and it might just drag you with it. Navigating life is like being on that treadmill; you're going somewhere whether you're walking or standing still.

The psalmist started by telling us that it's good to avoid bad counsel.

Name two influences on the way you act or think.

Is this influence positive or negative? Why?

The psalmist urges us to avoid the counsel of the wicked. *Counsel* is another word for *advice* or *wisdom*. If you go to court, you can get a counselor to advise you on how to proceed. Schools have guidance counselors who help students navigate their education.

Those are examples of good counsel. Here the psalmist says we're to avoid the counsel of the wicked. Wickedness speaks to the desires of the heart. Wicked counsel is a corrupting influence that steers you away from the presence of God.

We're surrounded by this kind of influence all the time. Whether it's from peers, magazines, or media outlets, the counsel of the wicked is rampant in today's world. If we're to follow God's path, we need to avoid worldly wisdom and stick to God's Word.

Identify some corrupting influences in today's world.

What kind of bad advice do these influences give?

Why do you think it's so easy to get off track in our walk with God?

The psalmist continued with a valuable piece of insight that has deep implications:

> *Blessed is the man*
> *who walks not in the counsel of the wicked,*
> *nor stands in the way of sinners.*
> **PSALM 1:1, ESV**

Notice that a pattern is starting to develop in the verbs the psalmist used. First we saw that it's good to avoid walking in the counsel of the wicked. Now we see that it's good to avoid standing among sinners.

How could you spot a group of people who are up to no good? What about their behavior might tip you off?

People who are up to no good may not walk up to you and try to get you to join them. Many times they have to be sought out and approached. Part of the blessing of not standing among sinners comes from not seeking trouble.

Notice the downward motion of the person on the negative side of this blessing. He started out walking but is now standing. His forward motion, signifying progress and life, has stopped, and he's now settling in and becoming complacent.

Don't let your walk stagnate; don't seek sinners to stand with. As you keep your eyes focused on the Lord, keep walking in the direction He leads you, and you'll find it increasingly easier to pass by sinners without joining in.

Have you ever seen someone whose forward progress with the Lord came to a halt after they joined the wrong crowd?

What kinds of temptations hit you hardest? How can you walk in such a way as to avoid them?

The psalmist's depiction of wickedness is almost complete. Read the next part:

> *Blessed is the man*
>   *who walks not in the counsel of the wicked,*
> *nor stands in the way of sinners,*
>   *nor sits in the seat of scoffers.*
> **PSALM 1:1, ESV**

The psalmist has demonstrated with a word picture the way walking in the advice of the wicked affects us. When we heed their counsel, we stop moving forward; when we stop moving forward, we end up sitting on the ground.

Have you ever seen a group of people who live just to make fun of people? You might have seen them in school as they cracked rude jokes at other students. Maybe they seem to thrive by stirring up controversy on Facebook. The word *scoffers* refers to people who mock someone or something. They're vocal and flagrant in their sin.

Why is joining mockery such a temptation today?

Why is sitting with mockers so much easier than walking away from them?

A downward spiral from lesser to greater sins occurs as a person disregards the Word of God. The second we start making allowances for little sins and tolerating things we know we should oppose, it becomes easier to make bigger exceptions for even greater sins down the line.

Even if you've taken your seat among scoffers, though, know that it's never too late to stand and start walking again. It may be hard at first, because our muscles get used to sitting and our hearts get used to sinning. But Scripture calls you blessed if you don't walk with sinners and scoffers.

Blessed in this verse doesn't refer to financial or physical prosperity. The ancient Hebrew expression translated "blessed is" refers to the blessings of covenant life and the joy of continually living in the presence of God.

In the past few years what blessings have you experienced in your walk with God?

How can you keep your focus on Christ as you keep walking?

The passage continues by telling us how to avoid the wrong path:

> *Blessed is the man*
> *who walks not in the counsel of the wicked,*
> *nor stands in the way of sinners,*
> *nor sits in the seat of scoffers.*
> *but his delight is in the law of the* L ORD ,
> *and on his law he meditates day and night.*

PSALM 1:1-2, ESV

To avoid the counsel of the wicked, the way of sinners, and the seat of scoffers, we have to set our focus on the "law of the LORD" (v. 2, ESV)—to delight in the Lord's instruction. It may seem strange to delight in instruction, but for the Jews, God's law was life itself. It kept them on the straight and narrow path, and it proved that God loved them enough to keep them from harm. The law was the boundary defining all the freedom that could be found in Him.

Christians delight in the Lord's instruction too. When Jesus tells us how to have fellowship with God, we have a clear-cut path to being made right with Him. It's not enough to scan our surroundings as we walk on life's journey so that we don't fall into a trap beside the road. We need to get God's Word inside us and meditate on it day and night. When we're filled with the Word, there isn't room to entertain the thoughts of the wicked. That's how being saturated with the Word of God will keep you from sin.

How committed are you to memorizing the Word of God?

Take a few minutes to memorize Psalm 1:1-2. Remember the progression of the one who falls away: walk, stand, sit. The mental picture will help you memorize these verses as well as help you stay on the right path.

WEEK 3

JESUS' TEACHING MINISTRY

START

Welcome to group session 3.
Use the following content to start the session.

Last week we examined Jesus' birth and upbringing.

What did you learn in this week's personal study that changed the way you view your walk with God?

Countless writers over the years have grappled with the question of what truth is. It's a struggle as old as recorded human thought. It was old even in Jesus' day. When Jesus told Pilate that He had come to bear witness to the truth, Pilate scoffed and asked, "What is truth?" (John 18:38).

Jesus said and did some remarkable things that were inflammatory in His time. He confronted a thriving religious system that claimed to bring people closer to God and declared, "I am the way, the truth, and the life. No one comes to the Father except through me" (John 14:6).

That statement feels intense even today. And it should. It's at once the most exclusive statement ever uttered and the most hopeful. This week we're going to look at some of Jesus' statements in their original contexts so that they can come to life in technicolor and become instantly applicable in our lives today, two thousand years after they were uttered.

Figuring out what truth is may be a philosophical exercise, but we don't have to resign ourselves to that. We can personally know the One who calls Himself truth and beckons us to follow Him.

Watch and discuss video session 3.

WATCH

The kingdom of heaven was the most important
concept that Jesus ever talked about.

The Kingdom of Heaven

1. A person—Jesus
2. A power
3. A place

Ways to Be Born Again in the First Century

- To be crowned a king
- To be converted from a Gentile to Judaism
- To be part of a bar mitzvah
- To be married
- To be ordained a rabbi
- To be ordained as a head of a rabbinical school

Jesus is using hyperbole.

There is a kingdom power available today for us to live in, to be under
the King, to be subject to the King, and to enjoy the benefits of the King.

When Jesus' will is done, His kingdom will come.

VIDEO SESSIONS AVAILABLE AT LIFEWAY.COM/FORGOTTENJESUS

DISCUSS

We often think of the kingdom of heaven as a place we go after we die. While it's true that heaven awaits those who believe in Jesus, reducing the kingdom of heaven to a future destination lessens its importance for us here and now.

How can you experience the kingdom of heaven now?

How does the kingdom of heaven affect your everyday life?

When Jesus taught about the kingdom of heaven, He used a metaphor that His audience readily understood but that may have lost some of its meaning for readers through the years as marriage customs have changed.

Read John 14:1-6. How does understanding ancient Jewish marriage customs help you interpret Jesus' words?

How do those customs help you understand the church's role as Jesus' bride?

What should we do as we await Jesus, who's coming back to take us to His Father?

The church is Christ's body among the people on earth. That means we represent Jesus, act on His behalf, and share His message while we wait for Him to take us home. Unfortunately, we often misunderstand the way we're to act toward others.

Brainstorm ways you as a group can function as the church in your neighborhoods and community.

45

READING PLAN

Read the following Scripture passages this week. Use the acronym HEAR and the space provided to record your thoughts or action steps.

DAY 1
Ezekiel 34:1-16

DAY 2
Ezekiel 34:17-31

DAY 3
John 10:1-18

DAY 4
John 10:19-42

DAY 5
John 14:1-21

DAY 6
Mark 8:22-38

DAY 7
Luke 9:10-27

HIGHLIGHT · **E**XPLAIN · **A**PPLY · **R**ESPOND

REFLECT

If someone asked you, "Why did Jesus come?" what would your answer be? Most believers would say He came to die for our sins, to bridge the gap between fallen humanity and Holy God, or to complete the prophecies made in the Old Testament. These are all good answers because Jesus certainly did all that. But none of those constitute the reason He came.

Jesus actually answered the question for us:

> *"My kingdom is not of this world," said Jesus. "If my kingdom were of this world, my servants would fight, so that I wouldn't be handed over to the Jews. But as it is, my kingdom is not from here." "You are a king then?" Pilate asked. "You say that I'm a king," Jesus replied. "I was born for this, and I have come into the world for this: to testify to the truth. Everyone who is of the truth listens to my voice."*
>
> **JOHN 18:36-37**

Today we're bombarded with many points of view and opinions about what's true and what isn't. When we watch the news, we see people on every side of every issue calling the other side's view fake news. It's enough to make us throw up our hands in frustration.

In reality, truth is something people have argued about for thousands of years. This isn't new, but it's something Jesus spoke directly about. In John 14:6 He called Himself truth. In Psalm 119:160 the psalmist wrote, "The entirety of your word is truth."

Even when it seems that truth is hard to find, believers know the One who calls Himself truth. He beckons to us and says, "Follow Me."

In what ways do you see truth being undermined today?

Search Scripture and read other passages that talk about truth. How does Jesus bear witness to the truth?

PERSONAL STUDY 1
TOUCHING THE HEM

Jesus was a master at making teachable moments out of interruptions, especially when the people around Him were annoyed by them and especially when
they were, by our standards, grotesque.

In Luke 8:42b-48 we read about a hemorrhaging woman who touched Jesus.
It turned out to be the most amazing interruption of her life. To understand the
way this woman's issue of blood would have been regarded in Jewish society,
we need to read a passage from Leviticus:

> When a woman has a discharge, and it consists of blood from
> her body, she will be unclean because of her menstruation for
> seven days. Everyone who touches her will be unclean until
> evening. Anything she lies on during her menstruation will
> become unclean, and anything she sits on will become unclean.
> Everyone who touches her bed is to wash his clothes and bathe
> with water, and he will remain unclean until evening.
> ### LEVITICUS 15:19-21

What's your reaction to this passage?

Why do you think ancient Israel had to be so cautious about coming into contact with blood?

To our modern minds these precautions may seem excessive and harsh. Calling
someone unclean for something they can't control feels unfair or unnecessary.
But remember that in the first century medicine was primitive at best and super-
stitious at worst. This is what the Talmud, a Jewish commentary on Scripture,
said to do if a woman was bleeding and couldn't stop:

Take of the gum of Alexandria the weight of a small silver coin; of alum the same; of crocus the same. Let them be bruised together, and given in wine to the Woman that has an issue of blood. If this does not benefit take of Persian onions three pints; boil them in wine, and give her to drink, and say "Arise from thy flux." If this does not cure her, set her in a place where two ways meet, and let her hold a cup of wine in her right hand, and let someone come behind and frighten her, and say, "Arise from thy flux."[1]

Excessive bleeding was physically dangerous, for a woman with that condition was perpetually unhealthy from the loss of blood. The people around her shunned her as unclean. This treatment took a toll on her mental well-being. Now consider the woman who came in contact with Jesus in Luke 8:

While he was going, the crowds were nearly crushing him. A woman suffering from bleeding for twelve years, who had spent all she had on doctors and yet could not be healed by any, approached from behind and touched the end of his robe. Instantly her bleeding stopped.
LUKE 8:42-44

Put yourself in the woman's shoes. Knowing what you know about the way the ancient world regarded her illness, describe her probable state of mind.

Have you ever been in a situation in which you were desperate for help? What did that desperation drive you to do?

Try to imagine the scene. This woman was bleeding and pressing toward Jesus with twelve years' unsuccessful attempts to be healed weighing heavily on her mind. She was desperate. But she had a glimmer of hope. Having heard that a rabbi who healed people was coming, she risked persecution from the thick crowd following Him for a chance just to touch Him. Reaching out as He passed, she was just able to touch the edge of His robe.

That's a dramatic image—even a cinematic one—but it's probably not entirely accurate. She was desperate, yes, but her grabbing the corner of Jesus' robe wasn't a last-ditch effort; she was laser-focused on it. Let's figure out why.

Numbers 15:37-40 explains that traditional Jewish robes were supposed to have blue tassels on their corners. Deuteronomy 22:12 reiterates the command: "Make tassels on the four corners of the outer garment you wear." These tassels were to constantly remind the Jews to obey God's commandments.

How do you think having reminders of God's Word would benefit you?

Do you have ways to help you remember God's Word throughout your day? List practical ways you can remind yourself of Scripture, such as posting it on the visor in your car or setting it as a lock screen on your phone.

The entire Old Testament is replete with references to the coming Messiah. For example, Daniel called Him "one like a son of man" (Dan. 7:13). Malachi described Him as the sun of righteousness:

For you who fear my name, the sun of righteousness
will rise with healing in its wings, and you will go
out and playfully jump like calves from the stall.
MALACHI 4:2

In its context this verse comes at the end of a particularly harsh book. Written to confront a thoroughly corrupted priesthood, the Book of Malachi would serve as the final words God spoke through prophets for hundreds of years. Yet the book ends with a glimmer of hope: judgment was coming, but those who believed in God would find joy and healing.

The term "sun of righteousness" uses the word for the celestial body; however, it doesn't refer to the sun but to the coming Messiah. When Malachi wrote that God would come with healing in His wings, he used the Hebrew word *kanaph*. The same word is used in Genesis 1:21 to refer to soaring birds. In Isaiah 6:2 it refers to the wings of the seraphim.

**Remember that Hebrew people think in pictures.
When you think of wings, what pictures come to mind?**

**If you picture a bird spreading its wings over its
offspring in its nest, what feelings are evoked?**

**How does picturing God as a righteous sun
with healing in His wings make you feel?**

With these references in mind, the Malachi passage takes on another shade of meaning. In a messianic context it suggests the Messiah would appear with healing in His "wings"—the corners of His garments. His arrival was associated with the healing and restoration of His people. And His healing was more than just physical healing. More important, Jesus brought spiritual restoration from sin and separation from the Lord.

Jesus, as an observant Jewish rabbi, would have worn a one-piece, finely woven, long-sleeved tunic with an opening for His head. He also would have had an outer garment called a tallit with tzitzit, or tassels, hung from the corners.

Notice how incredibly this background affects the story of the woman in Luke 8. By reaching out and touching the hem of Jesus' garment, she was saying, without saying a word, that she knew the Word of God and understood Jesus to be more than simply a healing rabbi. She believed Jesus was the Messiah.

**Are you convinced that Jesus is the Messiah?
If so, why? If not, why not?**

Read Luke's description of Jesus' encounter with the woman:

> *"Who touched me?" Jesus asked. When they all denied it, Peter said, "Master, the crowds are hemming you in and pressing against you." "Someone did touch me," said Jesus. "I know that power has gone out from me." When the woman saw that she was discovered, she came trembling and fell down before him. In the presence of all the people, she declared the reason she had touched him and how she was instantly healed. "Daughter," he said to her, "your faith has saved you. Go in peace."*
> **LUKE 8:45-48**

Jesus' question of the crowd wasn't an attempt to learn information. He was aware that people were accidentally touching Him all the time; he also knew who had grabbed the wings of His cloak. His question invited the woman to step forward into the light.

Scripture is full of questions that God didn't ask in order to discover an answer but to expose the heart. God asked Cain where Abel was in Genesis 4:9, not because God didn't know but because He wanted Cain to admit what he had done. He asked Job, "Where were you when I established the earth?" (Job 38:4), not because God wasn't aware but because He wanted Job to acknowledge His position in relation to God's.

Jeremiah 17:9 says:

> *The heart is more deceitful than anything else, and incurable—who can understand it?*
> **JEREMIAH 17:9**

When have you had to acknowledge the condition of your heart? What did this moment reveal?

The woman in Luke 8 thought she was incurable. She had exhausted every avenue the world offered to make her well, but nothing had worked. She was desperate and felt entirely without hope.

But the woman had faith. She knew the Word of God, and she knew the Lord would come with healing in His wings, not just for her physical condition but for the condition of her heart. She recognized the signs, heard of what Jesus was doing, and knew this was the One she had been searching for to finally make her perfectly well. As she sought Jesus in the crowd, she likely had one thought: *If I can just get to Him, He will make me whole again.*

And in return, she was greeted with the comfort that only Jesus could bring: "Daughter, … your faith has saved you. Go in peace" (Luke 8:48).

In what ways are our hearts, as Jeremiah said, deceitful and incurable?

What things does the world promise will fill the God-sized hole in our hearts?

Being part of the kingdom of God means completely readjusting our mindset, shifting from temporary things to eternal things. We stop looking for satisfaction on earth and place our priorities on things above (see Col. 3:2). We filter every interaction through the lens of a kingdom perspective because we see people as God sees them: people for whom Christ died. Jesus has made us new creatures, born of His Spirit, so we serve Him by fulfilling that new purpose.

Why do the things this world offers ultimately fail to satisfy us?

How is what Jesus offers different from what the world offers?

How will you respond to Jesus' offer today?

1. The Talmud, as quoted in R. Kent Hughes, *Mark: Jesus, Servant and Savior* (Wheaton, IL: Crossway, 2015).

PERSONAL STUDY 2
TO SEEK AND TO SAVE

See if you can fill in the blanks:

Zacchaeus was a _____ little _____,

And a _____ little _____ was he.

He climbed up in a _____ _____,

For the _____ he wanted to see.

You might have sung this song in Sunday School or in a children's Bible study about that wee little man Zacchaeus and Jesus' decision to enter his home and dine with him. Sometimes, though, reducing something to a song, especially a familiar one, makes us lose sight of what's actually going on in the Scripture text. What this encounter reveals about Jesus and the ways it still affects us today are deeper than you might realize.

What's something you enjoyed as a child—such as a movie, a song, or a book—that seemed much different when you revisited it as an adult?

As Jesus interacted with people in first-century Israel, He slowly revealed precisely who He was, often in ways we wouldn't expect. He used specific situations and phrases that caused people to realize on their own that He was the Messiah. It's as though people had a partial picture of a puzzle but were missing a few key pieces to fully realize the truth. Once they made that connection, it changed their lives.

Read the first few verses of Jesus' encounter with Zacchaeus:

There was a man named Zacchaeus who was a chief tax collector, and he was rich. He was trying to see who Jesus was, but he was not able because of the crowd, since he was a short man. So running ahead, he climbed up a sycamore tree to see Jesus, since he was about to pass that way. When Jesus came to the place, he looked up and said to him, "Zacchaeus, hurry and come down because today it is necessary for me to stay at your house."

LUKE 19:2-5

Zakkai—or Zacchaeus, as his name is translated—was probably under five feet tall, which was short even by the standards of the first century. As if his short stature didn't distinguish him enough, he was also a tax collector, which meant that he was the most hated man in town.

Whenever the Bible mentions tax collectors, it's always in the context of sinners—and for good reason. First-century Palestine was under the governmental control of the Romans, the most powerful political and military force up to that time in history. Rome frequently imposed harsh taxes on the citizens under its control and employed people from those regions to collect the taxes.

The Jewish people saw men like Zacchaeus as traitors of Israel because they worked directly for the rulers who oppressed them. With all the muscle of Rome behind them, Zacchaeus and other tax collectors could require as many as twelve or thirteen different taxes a year at any price they desired. To make matters worse, Zacchaeus was the chief of the tax collectors in Jericho, one of the most prosperous cities in Israel. Because he held a top position in this despised group, he was something akin to a godfather of manipulation, habitually sinning by stealing people's hard-earned money.

**Even if you don't have enemies, do you have
people in your life who rub you the wrong way?
How do you feel when you're around them?**

**How do you react when someone you don't particularly
like walks into the room? Why do or don't you generally
go out of your way to engage positively with them?**

Jesus stirred up a hornet's nest by inviting Himself into the home of someone the people considered to be a hardened sinner. To put this in context, imagine Billy Graham visiting a Wall Street investor who stole millions of dollars from ordinary people. The people weren't happy that Jesus was visiting him; Zacchaeus, however, had a different reaction.

Luke 19 shows us two different reactions to what Jesus did: one that shows growing disgust for Jesus' ministry and the company He kept and another that shows Zacchaeus's reaction to receiving grace and forgiveness. Read the next two verses:

> *He quickly came down and welcomed him joyfully. All who saw*
> *it began to complain, "He's gone to stay with a sinful man."*
> **LUKE 19:6-7**

This wasn't the first time, nor would it be the last, when Jesus associated with sinful people. Unfortunately, because we usually employ sanctified language to talk about Jesus, we forget just how amazing and scandalous this incident was.

Imagine if you had a boss who came up through your company but now skimmed money off the top of employees' paychecks. Anybody seen associating with him in a cordial way would be regarded suspiciously by the rest of the office.

This is the kind of risk Jesus took by publicly inviting himself to Zacchaeus's house that evening. In order to bring salvation to Zacchaeus, Jesus risked being associated with sinners in people's minds.

How do you think someone else would describe your reputation?

Would you consider yourself inclusive of people
who are traditionally thought of as bad?
How do your actions back up that claim?

In a lot of ways, we're shaped by the company we keep. If you want to know what you look like to the outside world, an easy way to do that is to describe your closest group of friends. In Matthew 11:19 Jesus is called "a friend of tax collectors and sinners." He wasn't afraid to be known for keeping company with heathens and turncoats, because it was heathens and turncoats He came to save.

So the religious elite and the crowd in general looked at Jesus' inclusion of the tax collector as something that wasn't positive. But notice the way Zacchaeus responded to the news that Jesus was coming to dine with him: "He quickly came down and welcomed him joyfully" (Luke 19:6). Zacchaeus was about to receive the most life-changing visitor he had ever known.

After dinner Zacchaeus stood from reclining on his side at the triclinium table and said to Jesus in the presence of the people gathered:

"Look, I'll give half of my possessions to the poor, Lord. And if I have extorted anything from anyone, I'll pay back four times as much." "Today salvation has come to this house," Jesus told him, "because he too is a son of Abraham. For the Son of Man has come to seek and to save the lost."
LUKE 19:8-10

What happened? Zacchaeus's life completely changed in the scope of two verses, and his language reveals that change. First, notice that he referred to Jesus as Lord (see v. 8), a term of great honor and submission that Jesus' own disciples used to refer to Him. Luke used this term throughout his book whenever a metamorphosis occurred in someone's life. For example, when Jesus instructed Peter to cast his net into the sea in Luke 5, Peter initially responded:

Master, ... we've worked hard all night long and caught nothing. But if you say so, I'll let down the nets.
LUKE 5:5

After Peter hauled in the catch, however, he dropped to his knees and changed his perspective of Jesus: "Go away from me, because I'm a sinful man, Lord!" (v. 8). The term *Lord* indicated that a transformation has occurred in Peter's heart.

Examine your life. What are the indications that you've had a life-changing encounter with Jesus?

How does a genuine encounter with Jesus change everything?

Second, notice that Jesus declared, "Today salvation has come to this house" (19:9). In saying this, Jesus was playing on the connection between His own name and the word *salvation.* Jesus' name in Hebrew, Yeshua, means "salvation." Perhaps with a smile Jesus agreed with Zacchaeus that salvation (Yeshua) had indeed come to his house.

What has Jesus delivered you from?

Some critics say if Jesus wanted us to know He was God, He should have come out and said so. The problem with this critique is that Jesus came out and said it all the time—but as a Jewish rabbi rather than as an American pastor would have. Let's zero in on Luke 19:10 so that we, like Zacchaeus, can see the Lord for who He is: "The Son of Man has come to seek and to save the lost." In the Jewish culture the term *Son of man* was a euphemism for the Messiah. This name comes from Daniel 7:13, in which the author wrote that he saw "one like a son of man" coming from heaven in a vision. When Jesus connected that title with seeking and saving the lost, he did something extraordinary. He made a specific connection to a prophecy every Jew would have recognized.

In the time of Ezekiel, an Old Testament prophet, the leaders of Israel (whom he called shepherds) neglected their duty to care for their people (their sheep). Much of Ezekiel's prophecy is a strongly worded chastisement of them. At one point God said, "My flock was scattered over the whole face of the earth, and there was no one searching or seeking for them" (Ezek. 34:6). Ezekiel continued:

*Thus says the Lord God: Behold, I, I myself will search for my sheep and will seek them out. As a shepherd seeks out his flock when he is among his sheep that have been scattered, **so will I seek out my sheep, and I will rescue them** from all places where they have been scattered on a day of clouds and thick darkness. And **I will bring them out** from the peoples and gather them from the countries, and will bring them into their own land. And **I will feed them** on the mountains of Israel, by the ravines, and in all the inhabited places of the country. **I will feed them** with good pasture, and on the mountain heights of Israel shall be their grazing land. There they shall lie down in good grazing land, and on rich pasture they shall feed on the* *mountains of Israel. **I myself will be the shepherd of my sheep, and I myself will make them lie down,** declares the Lord God. **I will seek the lost, and I will bring back the strayed, and I will bind up the injured, and I will strengthen the weak, and the fat and the strong I will destroy. I will feed them in justice.***

EZEKIEL 34:11-16, ESV, EMPHASIS ADDED

God finished this passage by saying, "I, the LORD, will be their God, and my servant David shall be prince among them" (v. 24, ESV).

Of course, at this point David had been dead for four hundred years. *David* here refers to the coming offspring in David's line. This is another messianic prophecy.

When we read the words of Jesus in Luke and recognize His allusions to Daniel 7 and Ezekiel 34, we find a subtle, sophisticated, and distinctively Jewish way for Him to make a bold claim: that He was the promised Messiah and that He was the saving God, the Shepherd of His sheep. He was claiming to be one with God, essentially saying, "I'm the one Daniel prophesied about in Daniel 7. I'm the one Ezekiel promised would come to rescue Israel. I'm here to seek and save the lost, and I'm starting with Zacchaeus. He was a lost sheep, and now he is found."

How did Jesus find and save you?

Why do you think the religious elite of Jesus' day was so quick to draw a distinction between saved people and sinners?

In what ways do we do the same thing today?
What are possible motives behind this tendency?

How can understanding your salvation in Jesus affect the way you interact with others, particularly those who may be considered bad or dirty?

WEEK 4

MESSIANIC MIRACLES

START

Welcome to group session 4.
Use the following content to start the session.

One of the most striking ways to think about God's relationship to His children is a wedding ceremony. Two people become one; two families are joined together forever. It's a moment of celebration and union orchestrated by God Himself.

It isn't a surprise, then, that Jesus' first recorded miracle took place at a wedding (see John 2:1-11). Ancient wedding ceremonies looked different than they do today, but the same principle applies: two people are united to become one.

**In what ways does a wedding ceremony provide
a picture of a believer's relationship with God?**

**What's a ceremony in our culture today that you could
use to illustrate how the kingdom of heaven works?**

When I was growing up, any claim one of my friends made was countered with "Oh, yeah? Prove it!" It didn't matter what we were doing; the more outrageous the claim, the stronger the demand that the claim be backed up with action.

Throughout His earthly ministry Jesus was essentially facing crowds of people who were making the same demand. If they were going to believe His claim to be the Messiah, He would have to prove it. This week we'll look back at first-century Jerusalem and examine the Jewish people's expectations of what the Messiah would do, how He would act, and how He could prove Himself. Jesus acted in very specific ways to demonstrate everything they could have asked for.

The question remains for us today: Do you believe Jesus is the Messiah? Why? And if He is, what are the implications of your belief?

Watch and discuss video session 4.

WATCH

Jesus' Fulfillment of Messianic Miracles

1. Healing a leper

2. Casting out a demon from a man
   who was deaf and unable to speak

3. Healing a man who was born blind

Jesus is saying, "There's only One who creates
something out of nothing, and that's God."

The Pharisees weren't asking about signs and miracles.
They were asking about messianic signs.

Do not underestimate the power of your personal testimony.

Don't ever discount how God will use suffering and pain
and trials and tribulations in your life as a platform
for the gospel to be preached to a lost world.

VIDEO SESSIONS AVAILABLE AT LIFEWAY.COM/FORGOTTENJESUS

DISCUSS

Whether Jesus is the Messiah is one of the most important questions we'll ever have to answer. In fact, it's so important that John wrote his Gospel for the express purpose of convincing his audience that Jesus was the Messiah so that we can believe in Him.

Do you believe Jesus is the Messiah? Why or why not?

If Jesus is truly the Messiah, what implications does that fact have for our lives today?

Believing that Jesus is the Messiah and that He's the only means of salvation immediately puts us at odds with an unbelieving world. Everything we believe about goodness, righteousness, and holy living is diametrically opposed to the pattern of the world.

How does a believer's worldview differ from an unbeliever's?

What arguments would you make to convince someone that Jesus was really the Messiah?

Studying Jesus' context helps us immensely as we engage in gospel conversations. It helps us understand the Gospel accounts and what prompted Jesus to say things the way He said them. It also helps us understand the proof Jesus gave about His identity.

How does knowing about the miracles that, according to ancient Jewish tradition, only the Messiah could do help you get a fuller picture of who Jesus was?

What has Jesus done for you that only God could do?

How can you include those blessings in your story of the way God has changed you?

Thank God for giving you the means to believe. Pray that members will have opportunities in the coming weeks to tell someone about what Jesus has done for them.

READING PLAN

Read the following Scripture passages this week. Use the acronym HEAR and the space provided to record your thoughts or action steps.

DAY 1
Leviticus 14:1-9; Luke 5:12-15

DAY 2
Matthew 12:22-37; Mark 3:20-30

DAY 3
John 9:1-17

DAY 4
John 9:18-41

DAY 5
John 11:1-27

DAY 6
John 11:28-44

DAY 7
Isaiah 35

HIGHLIGHT · **E**XPLAIN · **A**PPLY · **R**ESPOND

REFLECT

Sometimes it feels as though we barely have enough faith to make it through the day. Some like the idea of Jesus, but they don't feel they have enough faith to believe in Him. Some don't even know what having faith looks like.

In John 9 we see a man who was in an incredibly difficult situation. Born blind, he had no hopes of ever being able to see. Until one day, that is.

Jesus spit in some dirt, made mud, rubbed it in the man's eyes, and then told him to wash in the pool of Siloam. When the religious leaders saw him, they were amazed by the fact that he could see.

What happened next is interesting. The Pharisees asked him several times who healed him, each time getting an answer along the lines of "Some guy named Jesus. I don't know Him, though." Finally, after investigating and interrogating his family and friends, they asked him one last time in hopes of coaxing the answer out of him by claiming that Jesus was a sinner. The man answered this way:

Whether or not he's a sinner, I don't know.
One thing I do know: I was blind, and now I can see!
JOHN 9:25

This man didn't know the first thing about Jesus except that his life had been permanently changed after just one encounter with Him. He put as much faith as he could muster in Jesus, and that was enough.

You don't have to know the intricacies of theology to believe in Jesus. You don't have to know the answer to every question someone asks. All you have to do, like the man born blind, is to say, "I don't have all of the answers to your questions. All I know is that I was dead, and Jesus made me alive."

How has Jesus changed you?

PERSONAL STUDY 1
JESUS: GIVER OF LIFE

We learned in this week's video that rabbis knew only God could raise someone from the dead. Their logic was sound: if God is the ultimate giver of life, then He's perfectly able to give it again to someone who has died.

Read this account of a significant resurrection in John 11:

A man was sick, Lazarus from Bethany, the village of Mary and her sister Martha. Mary was the one who anointed the Lord with perfume and wiped his feet with her hair, and it was her brother Lazarus who was sick. So the sisters sent a message to him: "Lord, the one you love is sick." When Jesus heard it, he said, "This sickness will not end in death but is for the glory of God, so that the Son of God may be glorified through it." Now Jesus loved Martha, her sister, and Lazarus. So when he heard that he was sick, he stayed two more days in the place where he was. Then after that, he said to the disciples, "Let's go to Judea again." "Rabbi," the disciples told him, "just now the Jews tried to stone you, and you're going there again?" "Aren't there twelve hours in a day?" Jesus answered. "If anyone walks during the day, he doesn't stumble, because he sees the light of this world. But if anyone walks during the night, he does stumble, because the light is not in him." He said this, and then he told them, "Our friend Lazarus has fallen asleep, but I'm on my way to wake him up."

JOHN 11:1-11

Most people are at least anecdotally familiar with this passage. The raising of a dead man to life tends to send shock waves even through the minds of people who don't believe the Bible is true. In secular culture the name Lazarus is synonymous with someone who rises from the dead. We're interested, however, in the man who facilitated his resurrection.

Let's view this famous text through Hebrew eyes. As the text points out, Jesus learned of Lazarus's sickness before he actually died. Mary and Martha knew that Jesus, a miraculous healer, could save him if He got there in time, but Jesus did something that was probably frustrating to them. He waited two extra days before making His way to Bethany.

**Identify a time when you asked God
to do something like heal a sickness.**

**What goes through your mind when it seems
as if God is just sitting there doing nothing?**

Far too often we would like God to work the way a genie does: we rub the lamp, present our request, and have it granted for us before our eyes. Unfortunately for our desire to be instantly gratified, that's not the way God operates. Verse 4 of this passage is stocked full of truth we need to understand:

> *When Jesus heard it, he said, "This sickness will not end in death but is for the glory of God, so that the Son of God may be glorified through it."*
> **JOHN 11:4**

Even though Lazarus and those closest to him would benefit from what was going to happen, this verse pinpoints the purpose of the miracle they were about to witness: it wasn't for them but for the glorification of the Son of God.

We see this pattern throughout Jesus' ministry. He performed a miracle, people's eyes were opened to who He was, and that recognition inspired worship. In every miraculous instance the result was a deeper understanding of God.

What do you think the motivation is today for seeking miracles?

Is that motivation in line with the purpose miracles played in Scripture? Why or why not?

Keeping in mind the purpose of miracles in Scripture, why do you think Jesus didn't immediately go to save Lazarus?

Read what happened when Jesus arrived in Bethany:

When Jesus arrived, he found that Lazarus had already been in the tomb four days. Bethany was near Jerusalem (less than two miles away). Many of the Jews had come to Martha and Mary to comfort them about their brother. As soon as Martha heard that Jesus was coming, she went to meet him, but Mary remained seated in the house. Then Martha said to Jesus, "Lord, if you had been here, my brother wouldn't have died. Yet even now I know that whatever you ask from God, God will give you." "Your brother will rise again," Jesus told her. Martha said to him, "I know that he will rise again in the resurrection at the last day." Jesus said to her, "I am the resurrection and the life. The one who believes in me, even if he dies, will live. Everyone who lives and believes in me will never die. Do you believe this?" "Yes, Lord," she told him, "I believe you are the Messiah, the Son of God, who comes into the world."
JOHN 11:17-27

Remember, we're reading this passage through Hebrew eyes. Jewish tradition taught that a person's spirit hovered around the body for three days after death. It sounds strange to our modern ears, but there may be physical grounds for this belief. Sometimes, especially in the absence of sophisticated medicine, someone who appears dead isn't actually dead. After three days, however, even a comatose person who hasn't been given fluids and nourishment will likely have passed on, since that's about as long as an average human can survive without water. Regardless of why this belief existed, if Lazarus had gotten up just a day after he was presumed dead, his resurrection would have been credited to a misdiagnosis or a false report of death. Jesus wanted to wait until no other explanation than resurrection was possible.

By the time Jesus arrived, Lazarus had been dead for four days. Everyone around him knew this was the end; there was no chance of his coming back. Still, Martha clung to any hope she had that Jesus could do something, even if it wasn't that same day. Jesus told her Lazarus would rise again, but she thought He was talking about the final resurrection. Little did she know that Jesus had plans that would astound her and would prove her incredible confession in verse 27.

Jesus said He's the resurrection and the life.
What does this truth mean to you personally?

What did Jesus mean when He said those
who live and believe in Him won't die?

Read what happened when Jesus approached Lazarus's tomb:

Jesus, deeply moved again, came to the tomb. It was a cave, and a stone was lying against it. "Remove the stone," Jesus said. Martha, the dead man's sister, told him, "Lord, there is already a stench because he has been dead four days." Jesus said to her, "Didn't I tell you that if you believed you would see the glory of God?" So they removed the stone. Then Jesus raised his eyes and said, "Father, I thank you that you heard me. I know that you always hear me, but because of the crowd standing here I said this, so that they may believe you sent me." After he said this, he shouted with a loud voice, "Lazarus, come out!" The dead man came out bound hand and foot with linen strips and with his face wrapped in a cloth. Jesus said to them, "Unwrap him and let him go."

JOHN 11:38-44

Something happened that day in Bethany that was unexplainable by human reason: Jesus called out to an open grave filled with the stink of death and an air of hopelessness, and the man who had once lain there got up and walked out. Other than the fact that a man was resurrected from death and walked out of his grave, what's most surprising is the reason Jesus raised Lazarus: so that those looking on would believe that Jesus was sent by God (see v. 42).

The fact that we're still looking at this resurrection thousands of years after it happened means it occurred for us as much as it did for the disciples and Martha. For those of us who have found new life in Christ, what happened to Lazarus actually happened to us as well. Read what Paul wrote about the reality of every believer's resurrection in Christ:

You were dead in your trespasses and sins in which you previously lived according to the ways of this world, according to the ruler of the power of the air, the spirit now working in the disobedient. We too all previously lived among them in our fleshly desires, carrying out the inclinations of our flesh and thoughts, and we were by nature children under wrath as the others were also. But God, who is rich in mercy, because of his great love that he had for us, made us alive with Christ even though we were dead in trespasses. You are saved by grace!

EPHESIANS 2:1-5

What do "the ways of this world" (v. 2) entail? What does the world value and celebrate that runs counter to the gospel?

**In what ways do you see people
living according to that pattern today?**

Lazarus was dead in the grave, beyond all natural hope of coming back. No medicine could make him well; no ritual could bring him back. No show of sheer will could enable him to walk, talk, and breathe again. The same was true of us before Christ. We were dead in our sin. No feat of human endurance or display of human conceptions of goodness could give us hope of eternal life because we were dead, powerless under our own will. But miraculously, we were made alive together with Christ, just as Lazarus was.

Describe your spiritual condition before Christ.

What brought you to a saving knowledge of Jesus?

How has your salvation changed your perspective on life?

**How do your everyday actions change
when you know your life is a gift from God?**

PERSONAL STUDY 2
JESUS: PERFECT ATONEMENT

Even the most devout lovers of Scripture get a chill up their spines when they hear, "Let's look at Leviticus." To Western eyes, the book can seem tedious and almost hopelessly foreign. We find it hard to read; hard to relate to; and if we're being honest, totally outdated.

What we don't expect is to read Leviticus and get a richer understanding of who Jesus is, what He did, and how spectacular His free gift of grace is. Those are the truths we're going to discover today.

Leviticus 16 is only thirty-four verses long. Take a moment to read it. Record where the blood went and how the two bulls were used.

What do you think it means to atone for something?

Describe a time when you had to atone for something you did or when someone came to you to atone for something they did.

The Day of Atonement, or Yom Kippur, was the most solemn of all holy days on the Jewish calendar. On that day the high priest atoned—or made amends—for the sins of the people. Let's look at a few key points of the ritual prescribed in the law.

AARON FIRST HAD TO INTERCEDE FOR HIS OWN SIN. Verses 3, 6, and 11 explain that Aaron's attempt to atone for the sins of the people would be pointless if he didn't first address the sin in his own life. He had to remove his priestly robes (see v. 4), put on humble clothes, and publicly atone for his sin.

This ritual shows us that atoning for personal sin is more than simply saying, "I'm sorry." It requires humility; removing the selfishness that makes us want to say, "It's not my fault"; and taking specific steps to pay the price our sin demands.

How frequently do you confess your sin to the Lord?

What does humility before the Lord look like in your life?

FOUR ANIMALS WERE INVOLVED: A BULL, A RAM, AND TWO GOATS. One goat was to be slaughtered and its blood splashed on the mercy seat, the covering of the ark of the covenant. The other goat became a scapegoat that symbolically bore the sins of the people on its back. It was taken into a desolate place and released.

The first goat, used for sacrifice, provided the blood that stood between the imperfection of humanity and the perfection of God. Because we're sinful people, we deserve death. Graciously, though, God provided a way we wouldn't have to pay that price. However, something else had to die in our place. On the Day of Atonement, it was a goat. Its blood took our place on the mercy seat.

The other goat played an interesting role. The price for the people's sins having been paid by the goat that was selected for death, those sins were placed on the goat selected to be released in the wilderness. This goat thus became sin for the people and carried their sin far away.

Often we make light of sin by thinking it's not a big deal or weighing certain sins more than others. In God's eyes, though, all sin represents rebellion against His throne, a bitter usurpation of His rule that's punishable only by death. The gruesomeness of this ritual, which had to be performed every year in addition to the daily sacrifices, reminded the people of the seriousness of sin and the gravity with which it must be regarded.

Think about how challenging, even painful, these instructions must have been to carry out. What does this ritual indicate about how seriously God views sin?

How seriously do you take sin in your life?

Think of someone, perhaps in the news or in history, who has done unspeakable horror. Do you hate your own sin as much as you hate theirs? Why or why not?

THE CARCASSES OF THE BULL AND THE GOAT WHOSE BLOOD WAS PUT ON THE MERCY SEAT HAD TO BE TAKEN OUTSIDE THE CAMP AND BURNED UP. Someone also had to lead the scapegoat into the wilderness. When these people returned, they had to bathe; only after they were clean could they return to the Israelite camp again.

I've never slaughtered and burned an animal, nor have I convinced a goat to head out into the wilderness, but I can only imagine how nasty that work is. The act of paying for the people's sin was messy, smelly, dirty, and vile but necessary if the Israelites were to obey God's commands and dwell in His presence.

It's sobering to think that God's feelings toward sin haven't changed in the entire history of humankind. Sin—no matter how small—can be atoned for only with blood. And because of the greatest miracle of all time, we no longer have to engage in a system of sacrifice. The perfect sacrifice has already been offered on our behalf.

**How do you think the act of slaughtering animals
to atone for our sins would affect the way we see sin?**

**How can we maintain a serious view of sin in a time
when we don't have to engage in ritual sacrifices?**

Read this description of Jesus' sacrifice for our sin:

> *The bodies of those animals whose blood is brought into the
> most holy place by the high priest as a sin offering are burned
> outside the camp. Therefore, Jesus also suffered outside the gate,
> so that he might sanctify the people by his own blood. Let us
> then go to him outside the camp, bearing his disgrace. For we
> do not have an enduring city here; instead, we seek the one to
> come. Therefore, through him let us continually offer up to God
> a sacrifice of praise, that is, the fruit of lips that confess his name.*
> **HEBREWS 13:11-15**

For a student of the Word who wishes to understand Christ from a Jewish perspective, there's no better place to turn than the Book of Hebrews. Jesus stated that He didn't come to abolish the law but to fulfill it (see Matt. 5:17), and Hebrews helps us make connections to the Old Testament law that prove that statement true. Jesus didn't replace levitical laws like the one outlining the process to follow on the Day of Atonement; He completed them.

Notice the connections between Leviticus and the Hebrews passage. Like the blood of the bull, Jesus' blood was spilled to stand between our sin and Holy God. Like the scapegoat, Jesus, as the perfect, sinless sacrifice, bore the sin of humankind on His shoulders. He was crucified on a hill called Golgotha outside the walls of Jerusalem, just as the bodies of the sacrificial animals had to be taken outside the walls of the Israelites' camp.

This chart details some of the similarities between the Day of Atonement and Christ's sacrifice.

Day of Atonement	Jesus Christ
Aaron first had to intercede for personal sin (see Lev. 16:3,6,11).	Jesus was perfect and sinless. He didn't need someone to atone for Him.
Aaron had to rid himself of his priestly robes (see Lev. 16:4).	Jesus came to earth clothed in the likeness of a man (see Phil. 2:6-8).
The veil in the temple kept sinful people apart from God's presence (see Lev. 16:12-13).	Jesus' sacrifice tore the veil in the temple, opening God's presence to all people covered by Jesus' blood (see Matt. 27:51).
Sacrificial blood came between humans' imperfection and God's perfection (see Lev. 16:14).	Jesus' sacrificial blood stands between imperfect people and perfect God, once and for all (see Heb. 10:10).
The sins of the people were put on the goat, which symbolically became sin for the people (see Lev. 16:21).	"He made the one who did not know sin to be sin for us" (2 Cor. 5:21).
The person accompanying the scapegoat outside the camp washed himself before reentering the camp (see Lev. 16:26).	Jesus was taken outside the walls of Jerusalem to be crucified (see Heb. 13:12).
The bull and the goat used for sacrifice and bearing sin were taken and burned outside the camp (see Lev. 16:27).	After three days Jesus rose from the dead, having conquered our sin, and returned to be seen again in Jerusalem.

What similarities between the Day of Atonement and Jesus' sacrifice made an impact on you? Why?

Did any of them catch you by surprise? Why?

The Old and New Testaments aren't two separate books; the New simply completes the Old. In the same way, the gospel didn't begin with Jesus; He completed it. He's the ultimate good news—the final, permanent answer to the problem of sin that humankind started thousands of years before Jesus arrived on earth.

Whereas a goat's blood was once sprinkled on the ark to ritually appease God's wrath for a year and another goat took the guilt of sin away, both facets of the ritual were realized on the cross. Jesus, however, wasn't conquered by His death on our behalf. Rather, He conquered death and rose three days later, proving Himself to be the only One truly capable of paying the price for our sins once and for all and permanently bringing us into new, eternal life.

**Could you explain the gospel by starting in the
Old Testament rather than in the New? What
points and Scriptures would you include?**

**How does understanding the ritual sacrifice of the Day of
Atonement bring Christ's sacrifice for us into full, living color?**

**When the scapegoat was chosen, the sins of all the Israelites
were put on its head before it fled into the wilderness, never
to be seen again. What sin do you need to repent of and
have removed by Jesus' power, never to be seen again?**

WEEK 5

THE LAST WEEK

START

Welcome to group session 5.
Use the following content to start the session.

Last week we examined evidence that Jesus is the Messiah. In addition to fulfilling every piece of messianic prophecy, He also performed the three miracles said to be possible only by God Himself.

Why do you think it's hard for people to believe in Jesus?

Our culture is easily distracted. A thriving entertainment industry gives us endless material to consume, fads go in and out of fashion, and an unlimited amount of information is directly streamed to phones that fit in our pockets. We have to decide every day: *Which article do I read? Which game do I play? Which shows do I watch?*

How do you tend to be most distracted from the truth of who Christ is and His promises to you?

The object of our worship is revealed by the way we invest the majority of our resources—not only money but also time, attention, and effort. This week we'll revisit a time when people had to make a decision between two people named Jesus. They had to decide whether Jesus Christ or Jesus Barabbas was more important to them.

What those people decided tells us a lot about them, but as we examine the motives of their hearts, perhaps we'll find that we're more like them than we want to admit.

Watch and discuss video session 5.

WATCH

*Inaccuracies in **The Last Supper***

1. It is set in the daytime.

2. The seating arrangement is inaccurate.

3. The menu is wrong.

If we're not careful, we will allow the culture to help interpret the Bible.

If we're not careful, we can allow cultural
perceptions to cloud our biblical perspective.

Barabbas has a first name—Jesus.

Barabbas is a representative of the entire human race—a descendant of
Adam—versus Jesus the Christ, who is perfect and sinless and righteous.

VIDEO SESSIONS AVAILABLE AT LIFEWAY.COM/FORGOTTENJESUS

DISCUSS

Hermeneutics is a scholarly word for correctly interpreting a text, especially a biblical one. It involves looking at the context of a passage—both its place in Scripture and its place in time—in order to correctly extract its truth.

As with Leonardo da Vinci's painting *The Last Supper*, people often misrepresent elements of Scripture. Their misinterpretations or inaccuracies are sometimes accepted as truth.

What misrepresentations of Jesus or Scripture have you heard?

**How can we diligently remain faithful
to the original intent of Scripture?**

It's hard to imagine that a crowd of people would reject Jesus to free a murderer. Because their priorities out of line, they couldn't recognize the true Son of God. Yet we do the same thing when we act on our misconceptions about who Jesus is or how we should behave instead of using the Word of God as our behavioral compass.

How do we have to decide between Jesus and imposters today?

**Why is it sometimes hard to take a stand for
a position you know to be biblically sound?**

The world doesn't go to the Word of God for wisdom. It turns to cultural icons, popular conventions of thought, and arguments that sound good even if they're not true.

Even though we regularly miss God's standard, Jesus still took our place on the cross. We're rebellious people with rebellious hearts who want to be the lords of our own lives rather than enthroning Jesus. We're just like Barabbas—slated for death because of our rebellion—but Jesus took our place and paid the price for our sins.

**How do you think Barabbas felt when the crowd
called his name that day instead of Jesus' name?**

As you close the session, thank Jesus for what He did for us on the cross. Pray for wisdom and courage to stand for Him, even when it's difficult.

READING PLAN

Read the following Scripture passages this week. Use the acronym HEAR and the space provided to record your thoughts or action steps.

DAY 1
Matthew 21:1-11

DAY 2
Mark 11:12-33

DAY 3
Luke 20:9-19

DAY 4
John 13:1-20

DAY 5
Matthew 26:1-25

DAY 6
John 18:1-24

DAY 7
John 18:25-40

HIGHLIGHT · **E**XPLAIN · **A**PPLY · **R**ESPOND

REFLECT

The gospel is God's plan to rescue humanity from the bondage of sin. It's His sovereignty in action. Even when we're unworthy, unlovable, and uncontrollable, God's power is greater. Jesus' sacrifice is greater than even our greatest sin.

If God is sovereign and powerful enough to forgive sin, He's also in control of the smaller, more temporal situations we face day by day. Jesus demonstrated this sovereignty for the disciples in a particularly tense situation. They were on the Sea of Galilee when the weather turned and started pounding them with rain, wind, and terror. Most of them had lived their lives in boats on that body of water, and they had braved storms before. But this time it was different. Read what happened:

> *[Jesus] was in the stern, sleeping on the cushion. So they woke him up and said to him, "Teacher! Don't you care that we're going to die?" He got up, rebuked the wind, and said to the sea, "Silence! Be still!" The wind ceased, and there was a great calm. Then he said to them, "Why are you afraid? Do you still have no faith?" And they were terrified and asked one another, "Who then is this? Even the wind and the sea obey him!"*
> **MARK 4:38-41**

A common challenge to an understanding of God's sovereignty is the existence of storms like these. Sometimes life seems unfair, as if it's tilted away from our favor. We feel we're doing everything right, but for whatever reason, the hits keep coming.

But notice what happens in the passage: the disciples wake Jesus, who, without batting an eye, makes the storm calm. The point here isn't to show that Jesus always stops a storm when we ask Him; that's not the case. The reason for this miracle is what happened in the hearts of the disciples: they began to see Jesus for who He truly was.

Jesus reveals Himself to us in a thousand different ways every day; all we need to do is look up and see him there, never having left us at all, and trust that what He does in the midst of our storm will bring the Father glory.

When have you felt overwhelmed by a storm of life?

How does God's provision of salvation give you perspective on temporary, chaotic situations?

PERSONAL STUDY 1
TRUE WORSHIP

In 2003 film director M. Night Shyamalan began putting out trailers for a new movie. Because he had become famous directing thrillers that were runaway hits at the box office, people expected his mysterious new movie, *The Village,* to be a thriller that dealt with monsters in the woods. The trailers were ominous, but they gave away little of the story to come.

People were surprised when they got to the theater and found the movie didn't quite match their expectations. It was largely a love story with a sad twist at the end that revealed the monsters weren't quite what people thought they would be. *The Village* wasn't a bad movie, but it certainly wasn't what people expected. They had put their hopes in a mental image of what the movie would be.

**Describe a time when you built up an expectation
that turned out not to be quite what you envisioned.**

As Jews grew up expecting the coming Messiah, they had all sorts of ideas of who He would be. They foresaw a heroic figure who would come and free Israel from the oppressive Roman government through a magnificent revolution.

In reality, Jesus came to do something far greater. He came to free humanity from the tyranny of sin and usher into eternal life anyone who believes in Him.

During the last week of His earthly life, Jesus received the kind of welcome He deserved as He was entering Jerusalem, even if the people didn't fully realize what He was coming to do. Read Mark's description of Jesus' triumphal entry:

They brought the donkey to Jesus and threw their clothes on
it, and he sat on it. Many people spread their clothes on the
road, and others spread leafy branches cut from the fields.
Those who went ahead and those who followed shouted:
Hosanna!
Blessed is he who comes
in the name of the Lord!
Blessed is the coming kingdom
of our father David!
Hosanna in the highest heaven!
MARK 11:7-10

The Hebrew word *hosanna* is a plea for salvation: "Save us now!" The people were at the right place but for the wrong reasons. We know this because of their actions and their word choice.

John 12:13 includes the detail that these leafy branches were palm branches. Palm branches and the cry "Blessed is he who comes in the name of the Lord!" (v. 9) were associated with the Feast of Tabernacles—the remembrance of Israel's time in the desert after the Lord brought them out of slavery in Egypt.

However, the upcoming festival wasn't the Feast of Tabernacles; it was Passover. By simply saying hosanna, the people were declaring to God that they were tired of being oppressed by the corrupt leaders who occupied their land. They were asking for liberty, for victory. They didn't want salvation from their sins but rather salvation from Rome.

What do you think most people today hope to gain by coming to Jesus?

How have you seen Jesus misrepresented before?

In case we're tempted to judge the Jewish crowd for its shortsighted focus on freedom from Rome, we should consider that we frequently look for human leaders to deliver us from our temporary problems. A quick look at American politics will show that we're no different from the Jews in this regard.

It's true that the Messiah would come to bring judgment of His enemies, but Jesus had another more pressing issue: God's own people needed to be saved from the consequences of their sin. Jesus revealed His priorities in His first act on entering Jerusalem during Passover week. He didn't ride up with an excited mob to the Roman occupiers and toss them out. Instead, He headed to the temple. But before taking any action, Jesus did something that may seem confusing at first but that can reveal important information about the hearts of those who follow Him:

> *The next day when they went out from Bethany, he was hungry. Seeing in the distance a fig tree with leaves, he went to find out if there was anything on it. When he came to it, he found nothing but leaves; for it was not the season for figs. He said to it, "May no one ever eat fruit from you again!" And his disciples heard it.*

MARK 11:12-14

Fig trees bud around March or April, and interestingly, the figs bud before the leaves do. When Jesus walked up to a fig tree covered in leaves, he expected to find fruit since the tree appeared to be healthy. Instead, he found a tree covered in the outward appearance of health, yet it had no fruit. He cursed the tree because He was hungry and because the tree didn't provide what the leaves promised.

Record some characteristics that people who profess to follow Jesus should have. For example, how do they deal with adversity? How do they treat other people?

How well does your life reflect the characteristics you recorded? Place an *X* on the scale.

1   2   3   4   5   6   7   8   9   10
Not well   Very well

Why did you assess yourself the way you did?

Picture the sprawling temple in Jerusalem as a fig tree. It should have been full of fruit, but instead, there was nothing. It was all empty appearance, with nothing that could satisfy spiritual hunger. Despite its religious commerce and constant activity, the temple was filled with hypocrisy. Consequently:

> *[Jesus] began to throw out those buying and selling. He overturned the tables of the money changers and the chairs of those selling doves, and would not permit anyone to carry goods through the temple. He was teaching them: "Is it not written, My house will be called a house of prayer for all nations? But you have made it a den of thieves!"*
> **MARK 11:15-17**

Jesus was likely referring to His earlier teaching from the Sermon on the Mount:

> *You will recognize them [false prophets] by their fruits. ... A healthy tree cannot bear bad fruit, nor can a diseased tree bear good fruit. Every tree that does not bear good fruit is cut down and thrown into the fire. Thus you will recognize them by their fruits.*
> **MATTHEW 7:16-20, ESV**

We should keep in mind that this wasn't Jesus' first time in the temple. Three years earlier, at the beginning of His ministry, He had also entered the temple, made a whip of cords, and driven out the corruption that had taken root there. Now at the end of His earthly ministry, He returned to do the same thing. Nothing had changed.

What's hypocrisy?

Record an example of a hypocritical action.

How does being around someone who's behaving hypocritically make you feel? Has this person ever been you?

Arnold Fruchtenbaum described the corruption occurring in the temple like this:

According to the Mosaic Law you had the perfect right to bring your own sacrifice into the temple compound. However, it had to be without spot or blemish, and therefore it had to be inspected by the priesthood before it could be sacrificed. If you chose to bring your own sacrifice the priests, who were working on behalf of [the high priest], would simply find something wrong with your sacrifice. You had two options. You could go back home and get another one, and if you lived near Jerusalem that would be possible. If you lived up in Galilee, which was a three-day journey, six days round trip, that would not be practical. So in one part of the temple compound they had these stalls erected with sacrificial animals already stamped with the Sadducees' stamp of approval. You could purchase your sacrifice from them and they were sold at highly inflated prices. And the money went into the pockets of [the high priest] and his family.[1]

You may be able to imagine why these practices made Jesus angry. The problem wasn't selling things in the temple; it was the extortion and greed that drove the selling. The very roots of the system were corrupt.

That's how it is with our sin too. The problem is that our hearts are wicked. Because we're prideful and selfish, we do prideful and selfish things. Merely changing behavior isn't fixing the problem; we need new hearts. God despises actions without integrity and activity without worship, both of which were taking place in His house.

This reality was driven home when the disciples noticed the cursed fig tree the next day: "They saw the fig tree withered from the roots up" (Mark 11:20). The fig tree had been totally destroyed from the roots. This visual effectively foreshadowed not only the coming destruction of the temple but also the change that must take place in our hearts if we're to truly worship God.

Today as Western Christians, we can still glean wisdom from this encounter. Although we aren't Jews worshiping in the Jerusalem temple, we're often guilty of going through the motions in our worship. But Jesus reminds us that no matter how spiritual we may appear, our outward activity doesn't always reveal an individual's heart. Israel's religious leaders could speak the right words, but their hearts were miles away from God. May the same never be said of us.

How have you seen activity without worship in churches today?

How do you think God's children should properly worship Him?

What are some ways you're simply going through the motions in living a Christian life?

What changes can you make today to ensure that you're truthfully worshiping God?

1. Arnold G. Fruchtenbaum, *Yeshua: The Life of Messiah from a Messianic Jewish Perspective*, vol. 2, ed. Christiane Jurik (Ariel, 2017), 58.

PERSONAL STUDY 2
TRUE BELIEF

One day a girl I know, whom I'll call Allison, got a message from someone explaining that he had been in an online relationship with a girl named Maggie for three years. As they shared personal details about their lives, he felt as though Maggie was someone he would like to marry. He had tried to set up times for them to video chat or meet in person, but she always said something had come up that made it impossible.

The boy began investigating and found out that Maggie wasn't who she said she was. She had stolen all of the names, photos, and personal details from Allison, including the names of her parents, details about her life, her accomplishments, and major events from her past. He explained that Maggie had shared so much information about Allison that he felt as though he truly knew her.

It's a process called catfishing. Someone uses fabricated or stolen information to invent an online personality and interact with other people. But even though this boy had seen countless photos of Allison, knew her relationships with different members of her family, and knew about different events from her life, he really had no clue who she was; he knew only what Maggie had told him. While this boy knew a lot about Allison, she knew nothing about him. They didn't have a relationship at all.

In Matthew 7 Jesus described a similar one-sided relationship:

> *Not everyone who says to me, "Lord, Lord," will enter the kingdom*
> *of heaven, but only the one who does the will of my Father in*
> *heaven. On that day many will say to me, "Lord, Lord, didn't*
> *we prophesy in your name, drive out demons in your name,*
> *and do many miracles in your name?" Then I will announce*
> *to them, "I never knew you. Depart from me, you lawbreakers!"*
> **MATTHEW 7:21-23**

Who's the person you know best?
How did you get to know him or her?

What kinds of information do you know about each other?

**Why are you sure that you actually know this person?
What does your relationship with him or her look like?**

One of the most shocking parts of Jesus' story is the character of Judas. Some people have suggested that Judas was actually a good man who became disillusioned along the way. They claim he was a confused, card-carrying political zealot who grew impatient with Jesus because He hadn't initiated an insurrection against the Roman oppression.

Others, trying to discern the motive for Judas's betrayal, have suggested that he was misguided in his perception of the ministry. He sold Jesus out for a very small sum, a measly thirty pieces of silver, the price for purchasing a slave. It certainly wasn't a large enough sum to begin a military revolution. Consider that Judas had seen Jesus heal the sick, walk on water, give sight to the blind, and raise the dead. Having seen evidence of Jesus' power, he must have known that taking out a legion of Roman soldiers was something Jesus could have done in the blink of an eye. So perhaps Judas was hoping to force Jesus' hand, putting Him in a position in which He would have to confront the Romans.

If we're going to understand Judas's motives, we need to look at the three instances of dialogue with him that are recorded in Scripture. The first appears in John 12:

Mary took a pound of perfume, pure and expensive nard, anointed Jesus's feet, and wiped his feet with her hair. So the house was filled with the fragrance of the perfume. Then one of his disciples, Judas Iscariot (who was about to betray him), said, "Why wasn't this perfume sold for three hundred denarii and given to the poor?" He didn't say this because he cared about the poor but because he was a thief. He was in charge of the money-bag and would steal part of what was put in it.
JOHN 12:3-6

What outwardly appears to be a heartfelt desire to care for the poor was actually a ploy to hinder a woman from showing her extravagant adoration of Jesus. Judas was disgusted by the woman's act of worship.

**When have you seen someone do
the right thing for the wrong reason?**

**What do you think made Mary's
actions a genuine act of worship?**

**Why do you think Judas was so upset
by her use of perfume in this way?**

At this point it's the week before Jesus was to be crucified. His disciples had walked with Him through countless unbelievable scenarios as He transformed lives, walked on water, and raised people from the dead. At multiple points in His ministry, those closest to Jesus had professed their belief in Him as Lord. Yet Judas was upset by a woman who went out of her way to demonstrate how much Jesus meant to her.

The second dialogue is in Matthew 26:

When evening came, he was reclining at the table with the Twelve. While they were eating, he said, "Truly I tell you, one of you will betray me." Deeply distressed, each one began to say to him, "Surely not I, Lord?" He replied, "The one who dipped his hand with me in the bowl—he will betray me. The Son of Man will go just as it is written about him, but woe to that man by whom the Son of Man is betrayed! It would have been better for him if he had not been born." Judas, his betrayer, replied, "Surely not I, Rabbi?" "You have said it," he told him.
MATTHEW 26:20-25

Jesus' statement sent a shock wave through the hearts of His followers. But it's interesting that each of the men immediately doubted himself rather than accusing someone else. Each one asked, "Is it I, Lord?"

Lord isn't a typical term for disciples to use when referring to their teacher. The address is honorific, hinting that each of the men may have viewed Jesus as the Messiah. But notice what Judas said when it was his turn to speak. He said, "Surely not I, Rabbi?" (v. 25).

At the end of his three-year discipleship experience, Judas still looked at Jesus as a teacher, not as someone worthy of special honor. Even though he had heard the sermons Jesus preached, witnessed many of the miracles Jesus performed, and watched people be healed before his eyes, he didn't believe. He was one of the Twelve who were sent out to cast out demons and prophesy about the kingdom. He was one of the seventy-two who were commissioned and empowered to preach the good news to anyone who would listen and heal anyone willing to be healed. But none of this was enough to convince him that Jesus was the Messiah.

Why do you think people today can still miss Jesus even if they're around people who love Him?

How do you think we can discern between a "Judas" and a disciple?

Judas may have enjoyed Jesus' teaching and may have admired Jesus' ministry, but he was still in control of his own heart. He hadn't surrendered his life to Christ. He was still the captain of his own ship, seated on the throne of his heart. He was as close to Christ as a person could be, humanly speaking, and yet he completely missed out on a committed relationship with Him.

Is there any part of your heart you haven't surrendered to Christ? What step can you take today to surrender it to Him?

The final dialogue came just moments before Jesus was arrested in the garden of Gethsemane.

> *While he was still speaking, suddenly a mob came, and one of the Twelve named Judas was leading them. He came near Jesus to kiss him, but Jesus said to him, "Judas, are you betraying the Son of Man with a kiss?"*
> **LUKE 22:47-48**

In a final betrayal—both of his rabbi and of his true intentions—Judas revealed, in the ultimate way, his true colors. He may have had all kinds of justifications for his actions and may have been motivated by any number of factors that he considered good intentions, but at the end of the day, his actions demonstrated that he wasn't committed to Jesus or to the kingdom of God.

What does true commitment to Jesus look like?

If someone looked at your life, whom would they think you worship?

The real question isn't "Do you know Jesus?" The question that matters in the end is "Does Jesus know you?" If you know Him from a distance but haven't surrendered your life to Him, the only way you can be known by Him is to turn in repentance from your reliance on yourself and place your faith entirely in Him, trusting that only He can save you from the consequences of your sin and bring you to God.

Knowing Jesus as a disciple is more than just reciting words at the right place in a prayer. That's a very non-Jewish way of thinking about salvation. True discipleship requires obedience to Jesus. We understand that our lives now belong entirely to Him and that He rules and reigns over our lives. *Disciple* is another word for *student,* and when we're disciples of Jesus, school is always in session.

Over the past two thousand years much has been said about the person and the teachings of Jesus, and the majority of what we know is good and reliable. But we still need to study the Bible, dig out the truth for ourselves, and move beyond our cultural assumptions of who we think He is to uncover the Jesus who has sometimes been forgotten.

Is the Jesus we know the man who was born to a human woman, reared in a Jewish land, and raised in a Hebraic culture, or is He a Jesus of our own imagination who resembles an American pastor or a life coach?

More than ever, as followers of Jesus, we need to know our rabbi. We need to understand the man and follow the way of life He taught us to live.

How would you define a disciple of Christ in today's context?

Why is it important to know the true Jesus instead of a caricature painted either by our culture or our misconceptions?

How can you be sure that you know the real Jesus?

Record a prayer expressing your desire to truly know Christ so that you can obey Him more faithfully and display Him more accurately to the people around you.

WORDS FROM THE CROSS

START

Welcome to group session 6.
Use the following content to start the session.

Robby asked a simple question last week: Which Jesus will you choose? The crowd at Jesus' crucifixion chose Barabbas, but we still have the same choice in the twenty-first century.

In what ways do you see people choosing something other than Jesus?

If I walked up to you and said the words " 'Twas the night before Christmas," you could probably supply the next lines of the poem:

> *When all thro' the house,*
> *Not a creature was stirring, not even a mouse.*

Simply quoting one line would call you back to your childhood, perhaps sitting beside a fireplace or leaving cookies out for Santa. The poem evokes the Christmas spirit.

Rabbis like Jesus used the same technique. Because people in the first century didn't have their own copies of Scripture, they had to memorize them. When a rabbi wanted to call a student's attention to a passage, he quoted the beginning of it and expected the student to continue it. He might say, "The LORD is my shepherd" (Ps. 23:1), causing the student to remember not just the rest of the verses but all of the lessons he had been taught about what those verses mean, what it means for God to be his Shepherd, and the confident trust he could place in God to lead him even when life was difficult.

In this session Robby explores the way Jesus used this teaching method even from the cross.

Watch and discuss video session 6.

WATCH

The point is to know Him in order to love Him. The more you love Him, the more you want to obey Him. And the more you obey Him, Jesus will manifest more of His presence to us.

When Jesus is dying on the cross, He's not only suffering for the sins of the world; He's actually preaching a sermon.

Crimson is a picture of sin.

Jesus is taking on sin for all of mankind.

Even from the cross Jesus is saying this may look bad, but we are victorious in the end, and the world will know about this.

The separation between God and man is finally removed. The sacrificial system is done. The need for a yearly sacrifice for the atonement of sins is done. Jesus, in the finished work on the cross, has completed what God sent Him to do.

We don't need a high priest to go before us in order to atone for our sins. We don't need a temple to bring our sacrifice to. We don't need a wandering tabernacle in the wilderness.

VIDEO SESSIONS AVAILABLE AT LIFEWAY.COM/FORGOTTENJESUS

DISCUSS

**What's something you heard in the video
that made an impact on you?**

Understanding Jesus' words as He meant them to be understood will help us immensely as we finish this study and continue to discover more about our Savior and Lord on our own. Let's practice digging into a text together.

Read Psalm 22 aloud. What details foreshadow Jesus' crucifixion?

When a rabbi referred to the first phrase of a Scripture passage, his students would recall the rest of the passage, as well as the lessons they had learned from it. On the cross when Jesus said, "My God, my God, why have you abandoned me?" (Matt. 27:46) in Hebrew, it wasn't something the Romans who were crucifying Him would have understood. He wanted to teach His disciples one last lesson as He was dying.

**What do you think Jesus was trying to tell the people
around the cross by quoting from this psalm?**

Christ's crucifixion and resurrection are hotly debated historical events even in nonreligious circles. Everything in the world depends on them. If Jesus truly came back from the dead as He said He would, that fundamentally changes things. It alters common public conceptions of life, death, truth, and eternity.

**Paul said in 1 Corinthians 1:23 that his aim was to "preach Christ
crucified." Why is Christ's crucifixion essential to the gospel?**

**Do you think it's possible to get a complete view of
who Jesus was and what He did without understanding
the context in which He lived? Why or why not?**

**In what ways has your understanding of Jesus grown
over the past six weeks? What actions have you been
motivated to take in response to what you've learned?**

READING PLAN

Read the following Scripture passages this week. Use the acronym HEAR and the space provided to record your thoughts or action steps.

DAY 1
Psalm 22

DAY 2
Matthew 27:32-50

DAY 3
2 Corinthians 5

DAY 4
Galatians 5

DAY 5
1 Peter 1

DAY 6
1 Peter 2:1-17

DAY 7
Romans 12

HIGHLIGHT · **E**XPLAIN · **A**PPLY · **R**ESPOND

REFLECT

Throughout this study you've examined Scripture from the point of view of the people who wrote, witnessed, and participated in it. Putting Scripture in its proper context should have helped you understand what the Word of God actually says, as well as how to apply it to your life accurately and meaningfully.

As you've seen, when we seek to understand a term or a theological concept, a Westerner's first instinct may be to go to a theological dictionary or commentary. But remember, a rabbi went to God's Word. We can do the same thing. The rule of first use says the way a word or term is introduced in Scripture influences the way it should be understood in later passages. So if we want to think the way Jesus thought about a word, we should look for the first time the word is used in Scripture.

Let's take the word *faith* as an example. The first place the word is used that gives us our word for *faith* is in Exodus:

> *While Moses held up his hand, Israel prevailed, but whenever he put his hand down, Amalek prevailed. When Moses's hands grew heavy, they took a stone and put it under him, and he sat down on it. Then Aaron and Hur supported his hands, one on one side and one on the other so that his hands remained steady until the sun went down. So Joshua defeated Amalek and his army with the sword.*
> **EXODUS 17:11-13**

The root of the word *steady* in verse 12 gives us our word for *faith* or *faithfulness*. Walking by faith isn't just mentally agreeing to something; it's acting it out. By having Aaron and Hur on either side to help him when he grew weary, Moses was able to remain steady, or faithful.

The same is true of us today. Living a life of faith is something we were never designed to do on our own. We receive power from the Holy Spirit, but we also receive support from the community around us. As we remain in God's Word, let's also surround ourselves with people who can stand by us to help us walk faithfully as God has called us to do.

What's one thing you can do to walk more faithfully today than you did yesterday?

PERSONAL STUDY 1
A FAITHFUL RESPONSE

Once we encounter the truth in God's Word, we have a response to make: we either apply what it says to our lives or choose to ignore it. If we want to be faithful followers of Christ, we'll take the necessary steps to live out what He tells us in His Word. A Christian is constantly being renewed by the Word of God.

If you've spent any time around baseball players, you've probably noticed that they have a number of strange superstitions. One player found out after one of the best games of his career that he was wearing mismatched socks, so now he intentionally mismatches his socks. Wade Boggs can't play unless he eats chicken before the game. Other players go to great lengths to avoid stepping on the white-chalk foul lines when coming to and from the dugout.

These superstitions have less to do with supernatural influence and more to do with maintaining the idea of control over a situation. These players try all kinds of methods to keep their focus.

**What are things you do that help you focus
and feel comfortable in particular situations?**

First-century Jews were influenced by a lot of different superstitions. One of the more interesting ones mentioned in the Bible is in John 5:1-15. This passage takes place at the pool of Bethesda, located beside one of Jerusalem's entrances.

The people believed an angel occasionally came and stirred up the water. When the pool started bubbling, the first person to touch the water was healed of his or her affliction. For this reason a number of chronically sick and injured people lay around the pool day after day waiting for the water to stir and hoping they could be the first to get in.

Read a portion of the account in John 5:

After this, a Jewish festival took place, and Jesus went up to Jerusalem. By the Sheep Gate in Jerusalem there is a pool, called Bethesda in Aramaic, which has five colonnades. Within these lay a large number of the disabled—blind, lame, and paralyzed. One man was there who had been disabled for thirty-eight years. When Jesus saw him lying there and realized he had already been there a long time, he said to him, "Do you want to get well?" "Sir," the disabled man answered, "I have no one to put me into the pool when the water is stirred up, but while I'm coming, someone goes down ahead of me."

JOHN 5:1-7

We don't know what this man's sickness was. We can assume, however, that this man was fairly well known, having spent thirty-eight years in the same place. We can also infer something else about this man: his life was probably relatively simple, especially compared to people who carried everyday burdens in the outside world. He had to beg for money, sure, but his life was most likely a relatively comfortable one. He had a place where he was known and a convenient excuse to avoid leaving it. Perhaps he truly couldn't make it to the water—but the water, belief in which was just a superstition, wouldn't have made him well anyway. Perhaps he knew that being healed would mean leaving his comfort behind.

In what ways have you, like this man, become comfortable in your situation?

The Scripture passage tells us that Jesus realized this man had been there for a long time, but His question reveals that He perceived more than that. As He did with other people in Scripture, Jesus saw straight through to this man's heart.

103

Think about the scene. This man who had been lying in the same place for thirty-eight years, unable to get down to the water in time to be healed, was approached by a rabbi who was known to heal people of illnesses they had had since birth. "Do you want to get well?" (v. 6) was a question that carried significant weight. The obvious answer was yes.

What would this man have to give up by answering yes?

If Jesus walked up to you and asked you the same question, what would He know you need to be healed of?

Jesus didn't always ask questions that demanded straightforward answers, that is, for the purpose of learning information. Jesus' questions were usually devices He used to reveal the intentions of someone's heart. For example, He asked the Samaritan woman at the well to call her husband but not because He wanted to see him or because He wanted to find out whether she had one. Rather, He wanted her to confront the brokenness in her life. He asked blind men who were imploring, "Lord, have mercy on us, Son of David!" (Matt. 20:30) what they wanted Him to do for them. He knew, of course, but He was challenging them to determine what was most important to them.

When Jesus asked the paralyzed man in John 5 whether he wanted to be healed, He was trying to reveal the man's heart. Instead of the obvious answer, which would have been something like "Are You kidding? Of course I do! I've been lying here for thirty-eight years waiting for the bubbles so that I could possibly get well!" Jesus heard, "I have no one to put me into the pool when the water is stirred up, but while I'm coming, someone goes down ahead of me" (v. 7).

The man dodged the question and offered an excuse. But that didn't matter to Jesus. He simply replied, "Get up, ... pick up your mat and walk" (v. 8).

After being healed by Jesus, this man would have to give up the only life he had known for almost four decades. Look at your response to the previous question. If Jesus healed you of what you identified, what would you have to give up?

Apply this to a situation you may experience. Figuratively speaking, in what ways would "walking" after "lying down" for so long require you to have faith in the One who made you well?

It's no accident that Scripture compares living a godly life to a walk. Adam and Eve walked with God in the garden (see Gen. 2:8). Enoch walked with God and then was no more (see 5:24). Psalm 1 warns against walking in the path of the ungodly (see v. 1). Jesus calls us to deny ourselves, take up our crosses, and follow Him (see Matt. 16:24).

Walking with God requires leaving things behind, but it also requires putting our faith in the places where we plant our feet. If you're following Jesus, it's because you've heard His call to you: "Follow Me."

**When have you heard Jesus' call to put down what
you were doing, leave it behind, and follow Him?**

**How does it make you feel to know that your
desire to follow Jesus originated with Him?**

It's hard to leave behind the things we're accustomed to, but Jesus is prepared for our hesitancy. He's sufficient to satisfy all our needs, and He isn't going to call us to walk a path He hasn't already forged. If you need to leave behind certain things in order to follow Him, remember that He knew exactly what He was inviting you to do when He gave that personal, radical charge: "Follow Me."

Over the course of this study, we've come face-to-face with the real Jesus—the historical, miraculous, supernatural, real-life Jesus. Take a moment to reflect on your journey.

**What chain of events led you to participate in
this Bible study as a step in your walk with God?**

What are some misconceptions you had about who Jesus was, what He did, or what His words and actions meant?

How have those misconceptions changed during this study?

When Jesus met prospective disciples, He didn't ask them to explain finer points of theology. He didn't ask them to work miracles. He didn't ask them to put on impressive displays of mountain-shaking faith. He offered them His hand and simply asked them to follow Him.

We have the same offer today. It's an offer to put as much faith as we have in as much of Jesus as we know, take His hand, and say yes.

PERSONAL STUDY 2
WHAT'S NEXT?

Have you ever thought about what happens after your favorite stories have ended? Think about the end of *The Lord of the Rings*. Sam, Frodo, and company have just trekked across Middle Earth, have encountered numerous perils that threatened their lives, have seen more of the earth than any hobbit before them, and have finally made it back home. No detail in their lives would be the same as it was before they left home. Quiet little Bag End would be boring compared to the fires of Mount Doom.

What's your favorite book or movie?

**See if you can record what the next day
would look like after the story ends.**

As the events of a story change the main characters in real, permanent ways, a believer's story is changed by a genuine encounter with Jesus. As we examine our next steps—what to do after we've encountered Jesus in His Word—let's take a look at one of the most influential people in the Christian faith: the apostle Paul. We're going to study two texts: Paul's defense before King Agrippa II, who was the Roman ruler of Israel, and Paul's charge to all those who, like him, have had their lives transformed by Christ.

Read Paul's story as he presented it to King Agrippa:

> I myself was convinced that it was necessary to do many things
> in opposition to the name of Jesus of Nazareth. I actually did this
> in Jerusalem, and I locked up many of the saints in prison, since I had
> received authority for that from the chief priests. When they were put
> to death, I was in agreement against them. In all the synagogues
> I often punished them and tried to make them blaspheme. Since I was
> terribly enraged at them, I pursued them even to foreign cities. I was
> traveling to Damascus under these circumstances with authority and
> a commission from the chief priests. King Agrippa, while on the road
> at midday, I saw a light from heaven brighter than the sun, shining
> around me and those traveling with me. We all fell to the ground,
> and I heard a voice speaking to me in Aramaic, "Saul, Saul, why are
> you persecuting me? It is hard for you to kick against the goads."
> I asked, "Who are you, Lord?" And the Lord replied: "I am Jesus, the
> one you are persecuting. But get up and stand on your feet. For I have
> appeared to you for this purpose, to appoint you as a servant and
> a witness of what you have seen and will see of me. I will rescue you
> from your people and from the Gentiles. I am sending you to them
> to open their eyes so that they may turn from darkness to light and
> from the power of Satan to God, that they may receive forgiveness
> of sins and a share among those who are sanctified by faith in me."
>
> **ACTS 26:9-18**

Paul's testimony is presented for us three times in the Book of Acts, but this instance is the most specific and fully expounded. Let's observe a few facts about this text.

PAUL'S CONVERSION WAS PERSONAL. Everything about this text describes how personal an encounter this was. First Jesus said, "Saul, Saul" (v. 14). Repeating his name twice indicated the specific nature of this calling. Jesus' question "Why are you persecuting me?" (v. 14) indicated that Jesus was reaching out to him because of a personal action Saul was engaging in.

We know anecdotally and from Paul's own words what his past was like: he was an intense persecutor of the church of Jesus.

Describe what your life was like before you met Jesus.

Where does someone without Christ find hope
and meaning in the world? Why are hope and
meaning apart from Christ ultimately futile?

How did you first meet Jesus?

PAUL'S CONVERSION WAS POWERFUL. At this moment around the world, Christians are being physically, violently persecuted for believing in Jesus. Can you imagine what it would take for one of these persecutors to turn so sharply that he begins preaching about the resurrected Jesus? That's exactly what happened to Paul. He was persecuting the church because of a misplaced sense of piety, but his encounter with Jesus turned him around 180 degrees.

How are you different now after meeting Christ?

How is the way a believer sees the world different
from the way a nonbeliever sees the world? How
do you view hardships, setbacks, and struggles?

PAUL'S CONVERSION WAS PURPOSEFUL. Jesus saved Paul not just to add one more person to the number of believers or to stop the persecution of the church but to make him a tool for God's kingdom. The Lord said:

> *I am sending you to [the Gentiles] to open their eyes so that*
> *they may turn from darkness to light and from the power of*
> *Satan to God, that they may receive forgiveness of sins and*
> *a share among those who are sanctified by faith in me.*
>
> **ACTS 26:17-18**

As believers, we aren't saved *from* something; we're saved *for* something—specifically, to be servants and witnesses of Jesus Christ.

Why do you think many New Testament writers called themselves servants of Jesus Christ? What do you think it means to serve Jesus?

How is serving Jesus different from serving self?

What are some ways you tend to serve yourself instead of Christ?

Paul explained in depth the purpose of a believer's decision to follow Christ in this stunning passage:

*From now on, then, we do not know anyone from a worldly perspective.
Even if we have known Christ from a worldly perspective, yet now we
no longer know him in this way. Therefore, if anyone is in Christ, he is
a new creation; the old has passed away, and see, the new has come!
Everything is from God, who has reconciled us to himself through Christ
and has given us the ministry of reconciliation. That is, in Christ, God
was reconciling the world to himself, not counting their trespasses
against them, and he has committed the message of reconciliation to
us. Therefore, we are ambassadors for Christ, since God is making his
appeal through us. We plead on Christ's behalf: "Be reconciled to God."*

2 CORINTHIANS 5:16-20

As people who've had encounters with the living Christ, we've been given the
same ministry of reconciliation: to be ambassadors for Christ in a world that
needs to know Him.

**What do you think Paul meant when he talked
about "a worldly perspective" (v. 16) on people?**

What would it mean to have a heavenly perspective on them?

**How would a heavenly perspective change
the way you interact with the people around you?**

Paul mentioned that through Christ we have the privilege of not having our trespasses counted against us.

When has someone trespassed against you?

How do we typically behave when someone wrongs us?

How can we use someone's trespass against
us for the glory of Jesus and His kingdom?

As we interact with others, we should do so as people who have had their sins forgiven and who have the ability to introduce others to that means of salvation. Salvation can come through nobody else but Christ, for He's the only One who has paid the penalty for our sins—before we even committed them (see Rom. 5:8).

To be ambassadors for Christ, we need to transform our casual interactions into intentional ones. That doesn't mean shoving Jesus on people; it means living as saved people and, whenever possible, sharing a testimony.

What's meant by a testimony of the gospel?

Have you ever shared your testimony with
someone? How did the opportunity arise?

If so, how was it received? If not, what obstacles kept you from sharing it?

Sharing a testimony is one of the most effective ways to tell someone about Jesus. As you interact with people, listen to their stories. As they're talking, you can identify with problems they struggle with and connect their challenges to issues you've also struggled with.

Many believers don't know how to share a testimony. It doesn't have to be complicated. The easiest way is to break it down into three stages.

1. WHO WERE YOU BEFORE CHRIST? Ephesians 2:1-2 tells us, "You were dead in your trespasses and sins in which you previously lived according to the ways of this world." The first step in sharing a testimony is to describe yourself, as Paul did in his letter to the Ephesians, before you decided to follow Jesus. What was your attitude like? What did you struggle with? What were your emotions? Where did you place your hope?

Some Christians feel as though they don't have a dramatic story to tell, and others feel they've done things that will harm their witness. Remember, as Paul wrote, we were all dead in our trespasses. There are no degrees of deadness, for Jesus is capable of raising everyone to life in Him.

2. HOW DID YOU COME TO KNOW CHRIST? When the Philippian jailer asked Paul and Silas what he had to do to be saved, they responded with a simple answer: "Believe in the Lord Jesus, and you will be saved" (Acts 16:31). It doesn't matter where you've come from or what you've done; all that matters is turning from your former ways and accepting the free gift Jesus offers by believing in Him as the Son of God, who died for your sins and rose again.

When sharing this portion of your story, you may find it helpful to include answers to some of these questions: When did you understand the gospel? How did you realize that your sin separated you from a holy God? When did you confess that you were a sinner and needed Jesus to save you? How did you accept Christ's forgiveness?

3. HOW ARE YOU DIFFERENT NOW? In 2 Corinthians 5:17 Paul explained what happens when we come to saving faith in Christ Jesus: "If anyone is in Christ, he is a new creation; the old has passed away, and see, the new has come!" Once we're made new by Jesus after professing our faith in Him, something changes in our minds. We aren't perfect, but the focus of our lives switches from ourselves to Jesus.

When describing this stage of your life, you could identify ways you're different now that you're a Christian. How did your attitudes, emotions, and struggles change? How did your worldview change? How do you make decisions now?

Record your testimony.

Identify one person who needs to hear your story.

**Compose a prayer, asking God to orchestrate an opportunity
for you to share your story with that person.**

In this Bible study we've come to know more intimately the Jesus of the Bible, the Jesus who created heaven and earth, the Jesus who sacrificed Himself for us so that we could be reconciled to God. Take what you've learned and live as a wholehearted follower of Christ whose sins have been forgiven. Live as the light Jesus called His followers to be (see Matt. 5:14-16).

We've met Jesus. And meeting Jesus makes all the difference in the world.

LEADER GUIDE

GROUP SESSION 1
CONSIDERING JESUS' JEWISHNESS

To fully understand people, you must first understand the context they grew up in. What language they spoke, what customs they observed, what their society considered valuable, and countless other pieces of information contribute to our understanding of the things people say. In this session we'll explore the difference between Hebrew and Greek mindsets, and we'll use that distinction to help us better understand Jesus.

It's easy to operate from a mindset that reflects the culture we live in, especially when we talk about God. Jesus' culture often thought about God quite differently than we do.

Ask group members the following questions to get them to think about what God is like. They might respond with words like *omnipotent, powerful, Creator,* and *Lord.* Encourage them to answer as honestly as they can, even if they don't know how to describe Him.

What are some words you would use to describe God?

**Do those words bring to mind any specific images
for you? How do they help you see God more clearly?**

Remind the group that Hebrew culture thought less in terms of dictionary words and more in terms of images or feelings. Redirect your group's thinking by asking them to think of images that are associated with sense stimulations. For instance, the image of fresh-baked bread suggests an aroma, a visual picture, warmth, and an expectancy of eating something delicious.

**Think of a picture that describes God.
What do the characteristics of that image—
such as smell, feel, and sound—say about God?**

As we embark on a journey to rediscover an ancient Eastern rabbi as twenty-first-century Westerners, a useful starting point is to place ourselves in His context.

Why is it important to see Jesus through a Hebrew lens?

**What are some examples of Greek thinking (A or B)
and Hebrew thinking (A and B) in Scripture?**

In Western thinking we struggle with things that seem impossible. Hebrews don't have this same resistance. For instance, if you asked a rabbi whether he chose God or God chose him, he would answer yes.

Developing a common understanding is often the first step in bringing two different cultures closer together. By knowing how Jesus and the people around Him lived and thought, we'll be able to experience His teachings and understand His commands in a way that's both accurate and immediately applicable to our everyday lives.

**How do you think studying Jesus' culture will help us
better understand and obey His teachings?**

NOTES

GROUP SESSION 2
JESUS' CHILDHOOD

When we're getting to know someone, one of the first things we do is to learn about their family—where they grew up, what their siblings are like, what their parents do, what they did for fun in their hometowns. In this session we'll consider Jesus' background in order to understand His Jewishness and to develop a more complete picture of who He is and what He has done for us.

**Take turns sharing something about your childhood
that influenced the way you live today.**

As we week to know Jesus better, an important place to start is the context in which He grew up. If we know the culture in which He was raised, it will help us understand the images He chose, the examples He used when He was teaching, and the way people would have understood what he was saying.

**What's something about Jesus' teachings or actions that
you could understand better by studying His upbringing?**

Why is it important to know the culture in which Jesus lived?

Knowing where Jesus came from, the influences on His life as He grew up, and the day-to-day activities of the people around Him will bring His words and teachings into sharper focus.
Read these verses aloud.

*I also say to you that you are Peter, and on this rock I will
build my church, and the gates of Hades will not overpower it.*
MATTHEW 16:18

*Jesus said to them, "Have you never read in the Scriptures:
The stone that the builders rejected has become the cornerstone.
This is what the Lord has done and it is wonderful in our eyes"?*
MATTHEW 21:42

*As you come to him, a living stone—rejected by people but
chosen and honored by God—you yourselves, as living stones,
a spiritual house, are being built to be a holy priesthood to
offer spiritual sacrifices acceptable to God through Jesus Christ.*

1 PETER 2:4-5

**If Jesus likely grew up working with stones as His father
did, how does that detail add clarity to these verses?
Why is it important to think of God as a rock?**

Even as a child, Jesus understood the importance of growing in love for the
Father by studying and obeying His Word. Guide members to discuss ways they
can know God better through the Word.

What steps can you take to do the same thing today?

One of the most effective ways to grow in the Word is through discipleship—
an intentional time devoted to growing spiritually alongside other believers.

What does discipleship look like in your context?

**How can you help lead peers or coworkers in intentional times
of spiritual growth based on Jesus, the rock of our salvation?**

NOTES

GROUP SESSION 3
JESUS' TEACHING MINISTRY

Jesus said some controversial things during his time on earth, particularly when He called Himself "the way, the truth, and the life" (John 14:6). The world reacts negatively to this message of exclusivity. But as we examine some of Jesus' more difficult or surprising statements, we'll find what following Him should truly look like: not empty motions but full, rich life change.

We often think of the kingdom of heaven as a place we go after we die. While it's true that heaven awaits those who believe in Jesus, reducing the kingdom of heaven to a future destination lessens its importance for us here and now.

Being a resident of the kingdom of heaven means we've shifted our mindset from the temporal to the eternal. We recognize the difference between things that will last and things that won't. Guide members in a discussion that will point their minds toward eternal things—how they react to bad situations, how they respond when they're wronged, and how they can experience peace that surpasses understanding.

How can you experience the kingdom of heaven now?

How does the kingdom of heaven affect your everyday life?

When Jesus taught about the kingdom of heaven, He used a metaphor that His audience readily understood but that may have lost some of its meaning for readers through the years as marriage customs have changed.

**Read John 14:1-6. How does understanding ancient
Jewish marriage customs help you interpret Jesus' words?**

**How do those customs help you understand
the church's role as Jesus' bride?**

**What should we do as we await Jesus,
who's coming back to take us to His Father?**

The church is Christ's body among the people on earth. That means we represent Jesus, act on His behalf, and share His message while we wait for Him to take us home. Unfortunately, a lot of times we can misunderstand the way we're to act toward others.

As we strive to be the church and live as believers in a world that doesn't recognize God, we must remember to serve Jesus first, others second, and ourselves last.

**Brainstorm ways you as a group can function as
the church in your neighborhoods and community.**

NOTES

GROUP SESSION 4
MESSIANIC MIRACLES

This session presents members the opportunity to answer the question "Do I really believe Jesus is the Messiah?" for themselves. As we consider the messianic miracles, we'll understand why they were special and what implications they have for us today.

Whether Jesus is the Messiah is one of the most important questions we'll ever have to answer. In fact, it's so important that John wrote his Gospel for the express purpose of convincing his audience that Jesus was the Messiah so that we can believe in Him.

Do you believe Jesus is the Messiah? Why or why not?

Encourage honest discussion. If any members have doubts, make sure the environment is one in which they feel comfortable expressing their concerns.

If Jesus is truly the Messiah, what implications does that fact have for our lives today?

Believing that Jesus is the Messiah and that He's the only means of salvation immediately puts us at odds with an unbelieving world. Everything we believe about goodness, righteousness, and holy living is diametrically opposed to the pattern of the world.

As you approach the next questions, maintain the same atmosphere of honesty. These questions are easy to gloss over with answers that are common in church culture, but they're important. Make sure members who disagree with or are unsure about others' answers feel free to raise questions.

How does a believer's worldview differ from an unbeliever's?

What arguments would you make to convince someone that Jesus was really the Messiah?

Studying Jesus' context helps us immensely as we engage in gospel conversations. It helps us understand the Gospel accounts and what prompted Jesus to say things the way He said them. It also helps us understand the proof Jesus gave about His identity. Any claim we make is suspect until we provide proof. The evidence Jesus offered about who He was is proof that demands a verdict.

How does knowing about the miracles that, according to ancient Jewish tradition, only the Messiah could do help you get a fuller picture of who Jesus was?

What has Jesus done for you that only God could do?

How can you include those blessings in your story of the way God has changed you?

As you close the session, thank God for giving you the means to believe. Pray that members will have opportunities in the coming weeks to tell someone about what Jesus has done for them.

NOTES

GROUP SESSION 5

THE LAST WEEK

When the Jewish people were presented with a choice between Jesus and Barabbas, they chose Barabbas. In today's session group members will be challenged to answer the same question: Which Jesus will you choose? The gospel will be on full display as we examine how Jesus physically took someone's place on the cross. We'll come face-to-face with the mercy He shows us even when we don't respond appropriately to His sacrifice.

Hermeneutics is a scholarly word for correctly interpreting a text, especially a biblical one. It involves looking at the context of a passage—both its place in Scripture and its place in time—in order to correctly extract its truth.

As with Leonardo da Vinci's painting *The Last Supper,* people often misrepresent elements of Scripture. Their misinterpretations or inaccuracies are sometimes accepted as truth.

What misrepresentations of Jesus or Scripture have you heard?

**Do you think we need special tools or training
to read Scripture and understand it as God intends?**

**How can we diligently remain faithful
to the original intent of Scripture?**

Remind the group that studying God's Word isn't reserved for theologians or people with advanced degrees. Everyone in the room, no matter their age or educational background, is capable of reading Scripture and understanding it.

Looking back, it's hard for us to imagine how a crowd of people would reject Jesus Christ in order to free an insurrectionist and a murderer. Because they had their priorities out of line, they couldn't recognize the true Son of God. Yet we do the same thing every day when we act on our misconceptions about who Jesus is or how a Christian should behave instead of consulting the Word of God as our behavioral compass.

As you ask the following questions, be sure to keep the conversation on topic and prevent it from being derailed by any tangential doctrinal issues that may arise.

How do we have to decide between Jesus and imposters today?

Why is it sometimes hard to take a stand for a position you know to be biblically sound?

The world we live in doesn't go to the Word of God for wisdom. It turns to cultural icons, popular conventions of thought, and arguments that sound good even if they're not true.

Even though we regularly miss God's standard, Jesus still took our place on the cross. We're rebellious people with rebellious hearts who want to be the lords of our own lives rather than enthroning Jesus. We're just like Barabbas—slated for death because of our rebellion—but Jesus took our place and paid the price for our sins.

How do you think Barabbas felt when the crowd called his name that day instead of Jesus' name?

As you close the session, thank Jesus for what He did for us on the cross. Pray for wisdom and courage to stand for Him, even when it's difficult.

NOTES

GROUP SESSION 6
WORDS FROM THE CROSS

As the study comes to a close, we'll address the question "Where do we go from here?" As we study Jesus' words on the cross from a Jewish perspective, we'll come to understand what Jesus did for us, and we'll decide what to do in response to who He is and what He has done for us.

Begin by asking group members to recap what they heard in the video session and what they've learned in the study as a whole.

What's something you heard in the video that made an impact on you?

Understanding Jesus' words as He meant them to be understood will help us immensely as we finish this study and continue to discover more about our Savior and Lord on our own. Let's practice digging into a text together.

Read Psalm 22 aloud. What details foreshadow Jesus' crucifixion?

Focus your time on verses 1,6-7 and the images in 12-18.

When a rabbi referred to the first phrase of a Scripture passage, his students would recall the rest of the passage, as well as the lessons they had learned from it. On the cross when Jesus said, "My God, my God, why have you abandoned me?" (Matt. 27:46) in Hebrew, it wasn't something the Romans who were crucifying Him would have understood. He wanted to teach His disciples one last lesson as He was dying.

What do you think Jesus was trying to tell the people around the cross by quoting from this psalm?

Christ's crucifixion and resurrection are hotly debated historical events even in nonreligious circles. Everything in the world depends on them. If Jesus truly came back from the dead as He said He would, that fundamentally changes things. It alters common public conceptions of life, death, truth, and eternity.